Broken Brain:
Brutally Honest, Brutally Me

By
Dr Aria Nikjooy

Published by:
The Endless Bookcase
Suite 14, STANTA Business Centre, 3 Soothouse Spring,
St Albans, Hertfordshire, England UK, AL3 6PF

Available from:
www.theendlessbookcase.com

Paperback Edition:
Also available in multiple ebook formats.
Printed in the United Kingdom.

ISBN: 978-1-914151-07-1

To my beautiful wife,

If legacy was tangible, I'd buy you a truck full.

As it is, I hope it moves through people's minds

And reminds them how amazing you really are.

About the Author

My name is Aria Nikjooy. I'm a Paediatric Trainee Doctor working in Manchester. I've worked as a qualified doctor since 2014. I spend my days looking after unwell children from the second they're born to when they decide not to be children anymore!

I trained in Birmingham and moved to Manchester with my pregnant wife in the summer of 2017.

In November 2018 I was diagnosed with a rare brain tumour, sitting in my Cerebellum in the back of my head. It was operated on, blasted with radiotherapy, subjected to chemotherapy and was thankfully kept at bay, up till March 2020 when the same brain tumour came back. I had more surgery, more chemotherapy and then as a reward – another tumour regrowth in July 2020.

I've been at home on/off for the past couple of years, shouting at daytime TV programmes, writing in my notepad or typing on my laptop.

Part of my personal therapy of reading, writing and speaking out loud; I decided to write a children's fiction book so I could read it to my toddler son. Plus, a cancer memoir.

I am eternally grateful to all those that have supported me, physically, mentally and emotionally; regardless of how near or far you've been.

FOREWORD

Reader caution: This book contains graphic descriptions of some extremely unpleasant experiences.

Some of these descriptions may offend those with a fragile temperament, those with no sense of humour or those that use the phrase 'Golly gosh' without being sarcastic. If you think that applies to you then I'm sure there's something like Countryfile on iPlayer to spend your time on.

Some of the references are intended as a joke, most aren't.

Enjoy!

***

I'm not a very good man. I haven't helped nearly enough old ladies cross the road and I laugh way too hard when fat people fall over. Can't help it, I'm not a very good man.

However, I don't think I'm a very bad man either, if the world can be viewed such in black and white. I've never stolen anything, killed, cheated, or lied to anyone (that's a small lie). I've never spoken behind someone's back (that's a massive lie) or taken the name of God in vain (so many lies!). There may be others in this list, let's just say I didn't do them.

Despite that, I find myself at the sharp end of a cancer diagnosis. Do I deserve this? Does anyone? Have I pissed someone off? My wife? Darwin? God? Is there a God? If so, why me? Is this meant to be funny? Or a test? Is the answer to every question truly 42? Are there Copyright © issues here? How many questions do I have left?

And that's what I'm slowly learning as I travel through this process; no-one will answer those questions for you. It's not that no-one cares, it's simply that in a situation where you get an illness through bad luck, (as in I'm almost certain I didn't order this from Amazon) there often isn't anyone to blame. This memoir most likely won't have many direct or sensible answers, but at least it will acknowledge the questions. And that's all I really need, a platform to rant, rave and ask the odd question.

CONTENTS

PART 2

PART 1

SET THE SCENE

If you're reading this then you've either pissed someone off or you've been given the worst Christmas present ever. If you've gotten over either scenario then maybe you/someone you know can take some sort of solace from my story. Or learn a little about brain tumours or cancer or whatever. Just put this down if you're looking purely for factual information, I'm not going to explain how chemotherapy works, or go into detail about what type of tumour I was allocated. You don't need to know, and I don't have the mental capacity to explain it all. This is very much an example of how not to deal very well with life in general.

By the way, in the following stream of consciousness I may refer to **my** diagnosis or **my** experiences but in reality, whatever has happened to me has affected my loving family and should really be read as **our** diagnosis or **our** experiences. Semantics maybe but without my wife and son I would most likely be dead and you would be reading something far more cheerful than this.

***

Whilst I'm on my soapbox I want to make one thing clear: You don't 'fight' cancer, you 'survive' it. You can't fight your own body, it just seems to be this populist view that everyone with cancer suddenly becomes Sylvester Stallone and that you never give up until the cancer is defeated, preferably in slow-motion.

It's not a bad thing to be positive, but I'm damn sure being positive doesn't kill cancer cells. Doctors and nurses and radiographers and pharmacists and dieticians and physiotherapists and SALT therapists are the reason I survived. On top of all those amazing professionals and the treatments they provide, there's just blind luck involved, cells in your body just stop working properly or mutate and you get better or worse.

If another person tells me that a teaspoon of Turmeric a day allowed them to 'fight back' against their cancer, I'll choke them with a crystal...

THE BEGINNING

So, let's begin. I was born in Sheffield, I went to a good comprehensive school, got my Medical degree from Birmingham University, married my wife in Birmingham and then had my first child in Manchester. I then worked as a Paediatric doctor to fill in the gaps between nappy changes.

Then I got told I had brain cancer.

Would You Like Fries With That?

I can't remember exactly what the doctor said when we found out, all I remember is the word 'mass' and then something about calling Neurosurgeons. It could have been my doctor-instincts kicking in and zoning in on the keywords, or it could be that I'm a man and my first instinct when hearing bad news is not to listen properly. Who knows?

And why do people remember the exact words the doctor said at diagnosis? Like some terrible Twilight Zone version of events where everything seems to be alright, no matter how awful the diagnosis. As if every time people say the words out loud the cancer retreats a little, like a scared animal.

Well, I don't remember what the doctor said, but if I ever need to thoroughly depress myself, I'll ask my wife if she remembers.

***

The doctor in question in A&E did her job very well I thought; she took me seriously, arranged my scan the same day and gave me and my wife the news as soon as possible. I have no qualms about the process that got me to where I needed to be. Just a bit sore about the whole life-changing diagnosis thing.

Despite the hard work and running around going on: I felt numb. Anyone could have told me; my reaction would have been the same; just - numb. I think I remember asking some sort of boring question like 'when will I receive a phone call?' from whoever or whatever.

I didn't cry or swear. I didn't want to blame anyone. I didn't even want to hold my wife's hand, I just sunk into the chair, world shattered.

I just wanted to get my parking ticket validated.

Head in the Sand

Going back a month or so from diagnosis was when I started to notice things weren't right. If anyone but me is unlucky enough to read this, my one piece of advice is if you think you have a serious symptom then please speak to your doctor. Not leave it like I did.

I had horrible headaches, the sort that make you double over and beg for your mother's bosom despite her being miles away and you being twenty-seven years old.

Alongside headaches, my speech started to slur. I noticed it more when people on the phone at work would just say 'eh?' when I'd finished speaking. There's nothing more annoying than barking out a list of demands at three in the morning only for someone to say 'eh?' in reply.

I remember having a headache that literally brought me to my knees in the children's ward when my son was admitted to treat an infection. Me and my wife put my symptoms down to stress, well I did, and my wife made the mistake of listening to me. We had bigger problems, like who was going to buy more nappies or who would take the boy to nursery in the morning?

It was whilst I was working on night shifts that I eventually went off sick in November 2018. I'd hardly ever taken a day off work before then (although I do recall at one point having proper non-imaginary man flu and almost dying). More so than any thoughts of self-preservation, I remember feeling ashamed that I could be so weak as to go home from night shifts with a bleeding headache! Not turning up to night shifts is the doctor equivalent of doing a massive dump on someone's office desk – you just don't do it.

I've always felt a sense of contempt for those people at work who are 'sickly' and seem to have double the number of sick days as normal days. You know, the person at work who always seems to be off sick with 'tummy problems' and claims intolerance to fruit, vegetables, eggs, milk, inside, outside, having fun etc.

As someone who is supposed to be looking after other people for a living, I didn't assume the role of patient in a very dignified manner.

Biopsy Bonanza

Anyway, back to the story. I found out where I needed to be to have my biopsy the following day. For those who don't know, a brain biopsy involves being put to sleep and then a very skilled surgeon pokes around in your brain through a hole in your skull. They zone in on the bit that the scan said was a 'suspicious mass' and they take a bit of brain out for someone to look at under a microscope.

I felt fine(ish) after my biopsy and went home after a couple of days. I felt – ok. Reassuringly ok for someone who's had an alien probe in the back of their head.

At this point I didn't yet know if my 'mass' was cancerous or just a naughty, so-called 'benign' tumour that could be removed and never considered cancerous or 'malignant'. Turns out I wasn't so fortunate, and I was the lucky recipient of a malignant 'Grade IV Cerebellar Medulloblastoma'.

The message from the Multi-Disciplinary-Team of oncologists and surgeons was clear – take it out and cross our fingers.

Let's Play Operation

So less than a week later I was sat in an office receiving above news from my surgeon. When people describe out-of-body-experiences I sometimes think I was in the middle of one, looking down on this miserable bastard who has just been told he needs a huge operation and may not live to tell the tale. I could have shaken him by the shoulders and made him react, made him ask a question about prognosis or even ask about the operation. Instead, I think I asked if he'd shave my head at the back where the scar would be. Turns out my hair fell out later on anyway so what a stupid question that turned out to be...

Whilst I'm talking about my surgeon, I'd like to take this opportunity to say that he was amazing; informative, professional but concerned and had a kind face (it's funny what you consider important when your life is in someone's hands). Anyone who's worked as a junior doctor in this day and age will know what it's like calling Neurosurgeons at ten to five on a Friday evening but this man (and his team) were a cut above the rest. Unfortunately, you don't get to say that very much in the NHS today.

Cut to the chase (see what I did there, twice now!) and spoiler alert – I survived the operation. I was under the knife for a good seven hours or so. What those in the know might call 'a f**king long operation'.

Waking up afterwards was – as you can imagine – not a barrel of laughs. I remember throwing up almost immediately (or wanting to) and having loads of wires going in and out of my body. Need more details? I had oxygen up my nose, two tubes in my arm and a tube up my penis that collected my urine, so I didn't have to 'go' myself. Too much information? Thought so.

When thinking back to those first few nights after my operation, my mind wanders to images from artist's impression of Dante's Inferno. You know, descending through nine circles of Hell etc? Now when I read that out loud it does sound a little dramatic, but it does encapsulate how awful I felt.

Without going into much detail about what the cerebellum does in a normal brain, damage it and expect nausea/vomiting as a result. You'll have to picture that someone had taken a big ice-cream scoop out of the back of my head to remove the tumour plus some normal brain around it, a safety margin. Therefore, during my time in the High Dependency Unit, I vomited profusely and randomly. My head was constantly spinning and the only position I could put my body in to avoid vomiting was a kind of right-leaning laid-down contortionist-kind of setup.

I remember clearly shouting in the middle of the night asking for help. I'm not sure what for and I'm fairly certain it was some sort of panic attack but all the same, nurse after nurse walked past my room without bothering to help. Some Nobel Prize winner left the nurse buzzer out of my reach, just to taunt me (maybe I threw up on them at some point, I don't know).

Not being able to find a comfortable position sent me almost mad. The only way I can describe it is if you have an itch on the end of your nose and someone has tied your hands together. Then started to tickle you with a feather. And it's on fire.

Did You Eat All Your Vegetables?

Thus, began a long and depressing slog to my eventual discharge. With some action-packed scenes along the way of course. Well, 'action-packed' is subjective anyway.

I was moved to a ward with less nurses and doctors, more and more wires and tubes were removed from my body and I slowly began to tolerate people speaking to me again. The first dramatic act in my tragic comedy was my initial meeting with my Oncologist. This was the guy who planned all my scans, blood tests, radiotherapy and eventually chemotherapy. The first time I met him I was slumped in a wheelchair barely able to lift my eyes up from the pit I'd created for myself. I remember every time I would look up at his face my head would start spinning and I would get the urge to vomit. I'm not saying seeing his face made me vomit, but I did hold him partly responsible for it.

Not that I talk about her a lot or even recall her name, but I remember there being a medical student present at my first appointment. I recall saying hello and wondering if she knew that only a few years ago I was in the exact same position as her; a medical student watching a senior doctor deliver bad news to some other schmuck.

It was in that moment that I realised that not only was I a schmuck (have I spelt that right?) but I wasn't a doctor anymore – I was a patient. And a sick one at that.

What must that medical student have thought when she saw me being wheeled into the room, 'can we see someone who isn't a human vegetable please?' To be honest, describing myself at that point as a human vegetable was probably offensive to cauliflowers across the land. Have I been told off multiple times for using the term 'vegetable'? Yes. Do I care? No. Because in that moment (and many other dark moments) that's exactly how I felt and how I saw myself.

I appreciate this wasn't very fitting behaviour for a gentleman (careful) in my position but that was just the point; I didn't feel like a man or anything that could be useful to anyone. I'm not sure how long I didn't shower for after my operation – not that I cared – but when I finally got around to it someone had to help me. And I mean really help me: transfer me to the chair in the shower, scrub me with soap (apart from the bits we all know falling water gets to – maybe a discussion for another time) and rinse me in the chair. All I could say in my meek little voice was 'fank u'. I refused to let my parents help me wash in such a way. Even with half my brain missing I was stubborn as a mule.

VENOM

This is as good a time as any to discuss the concept of 'Roid Rage'. I was given loads of steroid tablets after my operation with the intention of shrinking my tumour. I know 'Roid Rage' is a term associated with people in the gym building up muscles, but I owned it all the same.

My wife is probably best placed to write this bit but the best way to describe me and my behaviour at this point was calling me 'Venom'. If you can't picture it, 'Venom' is an alien in the Spiderman universe that takes over a man's brain and makes him angry and aggressive. Google it and you might wonder what my wife thinks of the way I look but looking back, I think I agree with her about the personality bit.

Essentially, regular steroids can make you angry and aggressive as an unfortunate side-effect. And I had loads.

I was an arsehole, angry at everyone yes, but especially to my wife. I shouted at her about trivial things, I accused her of not having my interests at heart and I tried to hurt her with my words. I was angry. I was upset. Right now, maybe I'm trying to excuse myself by saying it was all the meds, but that can't be the whole truth.

She was my primary target because she was right in the firing line. She was there every day taking my shit, and that enabled the worst of me to take over. Don't get me wrong, I'm more than capable of being a total arsehole without the help of medications, but it almost felt as if someone was directing my words and actions.

An alien taking over my brain would have been a great excuse.

Would I have forgiven me were I in my wife's shoes? Probably not. But then I've already said I'm not a good man. Yes, I'm better now and yes this is probably a rubbish way to apologise to the love of my life, but it's all I can do. I'm not likely to perform in a Flash Mob (more likely never) or climb to the highest peak to proclaim my love. I'll just tap away on this keyboard and wait for her to find my 'Luv U Babe' tattoo hidden somewhere on my body.

CALL THE AMBULANCE!

Not long after my operation I was transferred to a specialist cancer hospital to continue my treatment. I was supposed to go home, recover and come back to have Whole Spine and Brain radiotherapy for six weeks, on an outpatient basis.

Instead, I was smuggled from one hospital to the other by ambulance one evening like a POW in wartime-France. I remember the journey clearly. The main reason I was being transferred as an inpatient was that my symptoms were so severe, I couldn't go home.

I was too unsteady on my feet and I was still throwing up everywhere – or least feeling too nauseous to get up and go anywhere.

The ambulance crew had to keep me laid down on a trolley with my head facing the right side. Any other position and I'd throw up.

Given that story you'd think the ambulance driver would take the transfer steady and drive nicely across Manchester, letting children and ducklings cross the road whenever they could. You'd think wrong.

I didn't vomit though, although I wanted to out of spite... I held my breath every time I thought they'd go around a corner and I tried to picture where I was going, as if that would help. Every bump and creak are locked into my memory. I'm sure the ambulance staff in my area do a great job but just then I could have done with an extremely elderly driver who thinks the speed limit is 20mph everywhere except motorways.

TIRED? I KNOW THE FEELING.

Because I was such a wreck, I remained an inpatient and started my radiotherapy in hospital, six weeks after my surgery. I might as well take this opportunity to discuss my physical issues, as they mainly stayed the same well after discharge.

Fatigue was/is a huge issue for me. But how boring is that... You know, that person at work who constantly moans about how tired they are to the point where you just want to drill holes in their head and see how it pans out?

Well now I'm that person and I hate it. My fatigue is real however, you know that feeling you get when you're out of breath after a fifteen second phone conversation? No? Well I hope you don't, because it's embarrassing and depressing. I have to smile and take a few deep breaths every time I walk down the corridor to my boss' office and speak to them, 'gimme a sec, I'm sure they've made that corridor longer over the weekend, puff puff'.

At the time of writing I'm no Mo Farah but I'm much better, able to walk a mile or so at a time. And then have a break, can't forget the break after travelling as far as a small asthmatic child...

I've tried to use an exercise bike. It's my parent's old bike that somehow seems to have made my father fatter over the years (sorry father, cheap joke I know) but I've gotten rid of that now too. Before my diagnosis I loved sport; I would play tennis once or twice a week (maybe less since work/baby reared their menacing heads) and I cycled to work whenever I could (but not in the rain or snow, not really into the whole deliberate self-harm thing).

Now exercise just makes me sad. Probably because I can't do what I used to. On top of my crippling fatigue my muscle strength just isn't there anymore, evidently because if you don't use it, you lose it. I feel like Icarus when he went too close to the sun and my tumour is a burning ball of fire, melting my wings when I feel like I can fly...

SICK TO DEATH OF IT

You know that feeling when you've drunk too many bottles of the wrong thing? Or eaten that piece of chicken even though you know in your heart you shouldn't? You remember the feeling, of overwhelming nausea almost forcing you to expel the contents of your guts? The acid bile you retch up after you've ruined the shoes of the person nearest you? That horrible taste in your mouth and the feeling of shame (not counting the ruined shoes)?

It's not your fault (unless it is) and yet you still feel bad when people crowd round you, pushing sick bowls in your face and looking concerned.

You know the feeling? Well imagine that feeling. Every. Single. Day. And every day for a long time I would vomit, at least once a day. I felt ashamed every time. It's the ultimate relinquishment of authority: you can't stop it when the feeling takes hold of you and you're utterly useless during it. When you're finished retching and spluttering and coughing and feeling sorry for yourself – you apologise. Why do we apologise after vomiting? Well, maybe not everyone does it but still, why do I do it?

After vomiting I would crawl up into a pathetic ball and apologise for puking/existing. I would feel helpless and hopeless and all words to that effect. I must say, the people that helped me were always helpful, occasionally I would throw up when no-one was around; I would summon help as soon as I could and sometimes just someone being there afterwards helped.

And I am sorry to anyone that I've vomited on, I promise I didn't mean it. Well, I may have done but then you probably deserved it.

Talking Out My –

Speech and language. I've addressed it as that because this is the realm of the Speech and Language Therapist, or SALT. I had no issues with my linguistic ability, but the mechanical side of things, the actual neurological processes leading to speech and swallowing, were something to be desired.

Speech was the first thing I noticed wasn't right when I woke up from my surgery. I was sprawled on my bed like a Geordie girl on her 21st birthday; 'Do you need some water?' 'Wader... wader plees'. The next few days got slowly better. I eventually got to the level of a Rocky Balboa Tribute Act, 'Adrian!!!'

I'm not sure what was said about me on the ward, about my speech and how to communicate with me. Hopefully nothing but I wasn't exactly brimming with conversation. Whereas before I would often use my words to get me out of sticky situations, (Rambo I ain't now), I was totally embarrassed to open my mouth. For fear of people not understanding me. Now you have to understand that every doctor likes to hear the sound of their own voice, it's an occupational hazard. My voice was slow, sluggish and difficult to decipher, which resulted in certain long sentences coming out like soggy pastry.

A good example would be me phoning my bank and going through 'voice security'. Before my operation, I had set a voice password, 'my voice is my password' I would say, and then I would be put through to a pleasant human being. Only now it wouldn't understand me, and I would just start raising my voice and swearing at it. I'm almost certain I didn't change the password to 'log me in you stupid bitch or I'll cut your hard drive into ribbons!'

I think not being able to speak quickly and with clarity made me even angrier with my lot. You know when a toddler tries to tell you they don't like eating couscous, but they don't know how to say 'couscous', or 'don't like'? The way their tiny face goes red and it looks like they're going to try and gouge your eyes out? That's frustration. Or they might be doing a poo in front of you, but in any case, I had similar frustration. I had the words ready to go in my head, like a missile being readied

– only what came out of my mouth was like a plastic bow and arrow, slow and pointless.

It affected me across the board; it made me less confident speaking to staff members, less confident speaking on the phone (good excuse not to have to call people I guess) and less confident speaking to my family. Even now at work in a busy hospital, I have to slow down, speak as clearly as possible and pray I don't have to repeat everything again.

Another toddler reference here (you wouldn't believe I have one, would you?) but there's nothing on this planet more annoying than issuing a command and hearing 'eh?' over and over. 'You bleeding well know I told you to put your coat on!' replied with 'eh?' 'Don't eat that Playdough!' 'eh?' 'Don't put your hand in the fireplace!' 'eh?'

Well, that's how I felt when I would ask staff in hospital to help me with something simple like opening the blinds or moving the table. I'd often get an 'eh?' and I'd have to repeat myself. It wasn't particularly their fault; it took me flipping ages to work out half of what Sylvester Stallone was saying in any of the Rocky films.

My family developed a method of understanding me, I'm sure of it. I didn't feel as if I was improving at all, but they seemed to slowly be getting me. I was close to going full-Hawkins and buying a tablet that I could programme with popular phrases like 'where's my f**king wheelchair?'

SWALLOW, COUGH, REPEAT

The other issue the SALT team deal with is that of swallowing. At the beginning I would often cough and splutter when food or liquid went down my throat. Mix that with crippling nausea and dry toast and – hey presto – vomit everywhere.

It was a brain-related complication that I just couldn't co-ordinate the parts of my mouth and throat to be able to eat and drink properly all the time. It's what it was, and it led to the SALT team recommending thickened fluids for me. Now I'm not going to mince words here, the thickened water through a straw was absolutely f**king terrible. I could spend a thousand years rewriting that sentence and it wouldn't come close to how accurate 'f**king terrible' is.

It's hard to describe as well because I remember not having a reference point for it myself when I first tried it. Gloopy water is all I got. And they tried different flavours of cordial in it, which helped a little, but was the equivalent of spraying cologne on a pile of dog faeces.

Over time I got better slowly, although I tried my best to lie to the SALT team whenever they came around. 'Coughing? Me? No Ma'am, I'm fine, thank you so much for asking'. Then they'd hand me a cup of water, say 'drink this' and I'd resemble a seventy-year-old man who smoked a hundred a day, coughing away like it was going out of style.

PIN THE TAIL

Dizziness/co-ordination. Did you ever play that game when you spin round and round on the spot and then you have to pin a piece of paper to a board, but your legs are all over the place and you just want to vomit? I have a sneaking suspicion that I know the name of that game...

Part of the cerebellum's job is to help with co-ordination; effectively any problems with this part of the brain makes you look drunk. And I looked as if I'd drunk a litre of Vodka every day. I sounded like that too, but content is much to blame for that.

'WALK FORREST, WALK!'

Walking was and still is a big issue for me. It's linked to my co-ordination and I'll start by saying, over time it has improved. As in I've gone from reaching for the wheelchair, to staggering around like a zombie from Michael Jackson's Thriller.

With the help of very patient Physiotherapists, I've effectively re-learnt to walk from my hospital bed. Coupled with my muscle loss from lying around in bed for months, it made my walk to the end of the hospital ward reminiscent of watching an Attenborough documentary where a horse foal has just been born, 'the young foal staggers around towards his first meal, will he make it? (Foal falls over) So close...'

I remember towards the end of my hospital stay I walked by myself (with hands ready to catch me) down the corridor and the ward receptionist cheered me on, she'd seen me struggle every day for God knows how long. She brought me out of my self-pity and made me realise how far I'd come at that point. She was annoying in a way because I hate any spectacle, but I suppose I'll be eternally grateful to her for her support. I guess that was my at-the-top-of-those-stairs-like-Rocky moment, 'duh duh duuuuuh, duh duh duuuuuh'.

Today, I'm in a much different place. Walking in a straight line for more than two or three metres is still proving to be a Herculean task, but I'm able to get about ok (as long as there isn't a cliff-face on either side of me). I've a sneaking suspicion that my shambling around at work may have tipped people off that I'm not firing on all cylinders — but then it's a hospital and loads of people have funny walks in a hospital. Not exactly Monty Python's Ministry of Silly Walks (Google it, please), more like step, step, stumble, step, step, stumble and grab the side rail, step, step, stumble in the opposite direction, step, step and then voila! Five metres down, only another hundred to go.

'Here's Aria!'

For months and months, I wasn't able to lie down and look in any other direction other than my right side. I used to dread going to bed in the evening, purely because for the first minute or so I would have to endure my head spinning around the room, my eyes flickering in every direction like Taz the Tasmanian Devil (bit of nostalgia there for you) and an over-riding sense of nausea would cascade over me, like an unrelenting wave. After a few minutes of hell, I would lie there staring towards the wall and tell my wife out loud 'I love you, good night'. My nearby grey sick bowl became a jealous lover, fighting for my attention.

I remember the first time I was able to turn towards the left side in bed. It took a long time and a lot of practice, but eventually I was able to stop myself from vomiting and a whole new section of my bedroom loomed into view. My wife said she woke up to find my face in front of hers (I always sleep on the right side of the bed) and she almost fell out of bed. I have that effect on most women...

Swimming Pools are for Fools

Recently I went swimming in a local pool with my wife and son. We messed about and encouraged him to swim about in his adorable inflatable life-jacket-thing. No son of mine's gonna swim in armbands like a weirdo...

I must have been having such a good time that I forgot what happens to me when I tilt my head back. Maybe I was trying to do the backstroke or maybe I was trying to show my son how an idiot drowns – anyway, I leant back and glanced up at the sky before my head submerged beneath the water. I immediately started a 'dizzy spell' and started to flop about like a fish. I didn't know where the surface of the water was whilst my head was spinning and later my wife told me my whole body was actually spinning around. She grabbed me and righted me as soon as she realised I wasn't joking.

I tried to laugh it off, but dammit I almost drowned. The young lifeguard must have been shitting himself watching me thrash about in the water, how can you drown in a pool this size? I tell you what, there's nothing like almost drowning to give you perspective on how crap swimming as an activity really is.

ALL THE BETTER TO SEE YOU WITH, MY DEAR

The list of all my bodily functions subsiding in front of me continues with my vision. The cerebellum has a big role in co-ordination of vision, you chop some out and the way the eyes work together and co-ordinate changes.

I began to struggle to find my place in a body of text. Looking at my phone would piss me off as I had to slow down to read anything. My eyes would wobble and wander away from what I was reading. Subtitles on the TV were a nightmare, my eyes just couldn't focus quickly enough for me to keep up with them. Have you ever turned on the subtitles on the morning news? Lots of different colours, places, different people talking hurriedly into microphones etc? Well, that was my idea of hell, like someone grabbing your head from the front and shaking it like the Macarena.

I was duly referred to the eye doctors who passed me about like a hot potato. I think I saw three different consultants; one referred me to his colleague about ten minutes after meeting me, one prescribed me a few different tablets (which turned out to be as useful as eating M&Ms) and another made me do another eye test. This eye test resulted in me wearing glasses, but at a very weak prescription – I don't need them for driving, operating heavy machinery or defusing a roadside IED. Essentially, they incidentally picked up that I needed glasses for occasional use – my original problem persists and typing out these words is involving a fair amount of ocular exertion.

I mainly use my glasses for reading and writing to avoid my eyes getting tired. They're a very simple design (free on the NHS, boom) and when I saw myself wearing them at work in a mirror, I did a double take. In front of me was a fifty-year old lesbian librarian. With thinning hair. And a beard. And a shirt that looks like a small child ironed it. How have I been allowed to leave the house like this? This is my wife's fault.

Can't complain though really, I can still see, lots of brain tumours render people blind or worse. Despite looking more intelligent with glasses, I am categorically not more so. My minor inconveniences are slowly improving with time and, like I said before, I can't really complain. I can still order garbage from the internet – apologies to my wife – and watch South Park whenever I want – apologies to my wife, again.

Radio Ga Ga

Have you seen 'The Man in the Iron Mask'? Basically, Leonardo Di Caprio has an identical twin brother who has to wear a fitted iron mask to hide his identity from the world. The irony of the mask (see what I did there) is that Di Caprio is such a handsome individual. I don't recall being a good-looking Oscar winner (last time I checked) and yet I had a similarly sinister plastic mask fitted in order to have my radiotherapy. To pin my body and head in place to make sure they didn't miss the brain and fry my eyeballs by accident.

The fitting of the mask was weird, they moulded this special plastic over my head and face, with the intention of keeping me still as a corpse. Then they tattooed some spots on various points of my body, which enabled the technicians to line my body up with the radiotherapy machine. So yeh mother, I went and got tattoos without asking permission, so there.

***

The radiotherapy itself was relentless. I had thirty fractions, which effectively meant I had radiotherapy everyday Monday to Friday for six weeks with 'weekends off'. Doesn't sound so bad, took about an hour and the radiotherapy suite was in the same hospital.

The actual radiotherapy itself involved me lying flat, face up as I was slowly inserted into the oversized whirring donut machine. It looks similar to an MRI or CT scan except for the radiotherapy robot arm thing was on hand to ominously circle my body and blast me with radiation periodically. I had my mask on so I couldn't see much but I got other sensations, such as a really weird boiled broccoli smell, pretty much every day. You read that right, weird but annoyingly consistent. I like broccoli, but to this day I still struggle with the idea that if you fry the human brain, it might smell like broccoli. Ew.

'Suite' makes it sound like a damn spa doesn't it? 'Time for your radiotherapy sir. Please lie down, face up on this hard death-slab plinth and I'll put this plastic mask thing over you. If you feel sick, please don't move because a) you won't be able to anyway because we're going to pin you down with the mask and b) you'll mess up the treatment if you do and we'll end up blasting the wrong parts of your brain with radiation'. Like a man using a urinal after too many drinks (fellas might know where I'm coming from).

My memory is fuzzy but I'm fairly certain no-one said that to me. Doesn't make it less true though. The main issue for me was lying down, face up. Like every night at that point, it would send the world spinning around me, my eyes would flicker like my batteries were about to run out of juice and I would get a wave of nausea. In the first few sessions this wave would produce a sea of vomit all over the radiotherapy table and floor. Or the sick bowl on the way back to the ward. Or anywhere near my bed on the ward. What I'm trying to say is it wiped me out for hours after the actual radiotherapy and made me feel sick as a dog. And it was every day, more or less, for six weeks...

I was the sickest patient in that damn spa. All the other patients were happily sat there in their coats (well not happily, they did have cancer of some sort...) and for a good few weeks I was wheeled down lying still as I could on a trolley, in my pyjamas (being naked in my bed might have killed off those in the waiting room).

After a while I graduated to being wheeled down in my wheelchair. Nothing makes you feel more like livestock than a wheelchair ride in a hospital – the way I carried on throwing up all the time and moaning I'm sure I was close to being made into a selection of steaks.

My daily appointments got earlier and earlier. One excuse was that I seemed to be better first thing in the morning and getting the treatment over and done with meant I could recover during the day. The other excuse was if I get back early enough from radiotherapy then I can watch Homes Under the Hammer on the TV. Silver linings and that.

WHURS ME HUR?

You know that scene at the beginning of Michael Jackson's Thriller (yes, I am using that video as reference again – rude not to) where Michael turns from a teenager into a werewolf? He grows loads of hair and shouts 'go away!' to his girlfriend. Well, the same thing happened to me, except I didn't shout 'go away' to anyone, I didn't turn into a werewolf and my hair actually fell out. Soooo, actually my situation was pretty much nothing like in that video, but maybe I just love that video and wanted you to remember/watch it again!

One morning I woke up in my hospital bed, ran my hand though my hair and almost wet myself. In my hand was a clump of hair and my pillow was covered with it. It looked like Cousin Itt had a fight with a lawnmower – and lost.

I admit, it took me by surprise – I just assumed it would be chemotherapy that made me lose my hair, but it was that damn radiotherapy. I just forgot that radiotherapy could do that to you.

The next couple of days more and more fell out, I can't find any photos of it, so I guess my family took pity on me and kept the paparazzi at bay. Eventually I gave in and my brother shaved my head completely for me to get 'the full experience'. You might think that would be a touching moment that would bring together two men in a single experience?

Nah. I just whined like a little girl when he went near the scar on the back of my head. I'm thankful to him though, if he ever needs me to shave all his hair off, I'll be there in a jiffy.

Flash forward in time and my hair is starting to grow back, it's thinner now and not as curly but it's not a wig and I still don't care what I look like really.

DING DONG, THE WITCH IS DEAD

I think I walked to the radiotherapy suite on my own two feet once or twice. Out of thirty visits that's a pretty pathetic return. The most poignant thing I remember is that stupid bell in the corridor on the way to the spa. It was designed to be rung by patients once they had finished their radiotherapy treatment, 'I'm still alive' kind of thing. I just saw it as depressing, 'why can't I ring the damn bell'? When I eventually got to ring it, no-one was around apart from my family.

Therefore, I felt embarrassed and rang it quickly, hoping to avoid any one awkwardly clapping (I hate clapping, it's fine for my toddler but as an adult I don't need people flapping their arms at me for validation).

Why was I embarrassed? Now, I'm not such a miserable bastard that I can't be happy for someone who completes their treatment and hopefully goes on to make a full recovery. I guess I was just unhappy with my own lot and wanted to pass through the gates undetected. The end of radiotherapy for me, was simply heralding the start of the next chapter....

I FAILED

Within the cancer hospital I first spent some time on a four-bedded bay before I was moved to my own room. Now, I'm about to be exceptionally rude about the other patients, but rather than me just saying I don't care, I want to make it clear that most of these thoughts and feelings were spawned from a dark place; I wasn't myself and I wasn't exactly in a kissing/hugging mood at the time. Although I'm no longer in possession of these obnoxious opinions, I feel it's important to acknowledge where my head was at the time.

Also, there's a very real possibility all/some of those patients could be dead by now. Which would make me a true asshole but hey, it's probably my parent's fault.

So yes, there's nothing like listening to other people prattle on about their lives when you're trying to sleep on an uncomfortable hospital bed. Multiple patients came and went on my ward, over time I would listen, and I learnt about their lives – their illnesses, treatments and what happened to them along the way to land them in a hospital bed. I learnt about their wives/girlfriends, I learnt about their myriad of medications, I learnt about their outlook on love, life and cancer. All from behind my magic NHS bedside curtain.

I just didn't give a f**k.

I didn't speak up, tell my story or even confess that I myself was a doctor and that half the nonsense coming out of their mouths I could help explain. Now, I feel awful. I genuinely could have helped them, some of them had straightforward questions about medications that I could have answered for them. I could've made them feel better by them looking at how pale, thin and pathetic I looked.

But I just checked my curtain was across and stayed quiet. I sat there and listened to their soul-destroying stories and just felt even more sorry for myself. I didn't much feel like talking to anyone to be fair. I was still desperately disappointed with the quality of my own speech.

It still doesn't excuse my actions, I had the opportunity to just say hello, sit and listen and I failed to do that. I failed as someone who knew a little (lamentably little) science, I failed as a fellow patient and I failed as a human being.

A lot of horrible stuff happened to me; it can't be disputed − but it doesn't mean I don't deserve at least some of it.

***

One guy had a genuine sad story about how his cancer had come back and he was basically riddled. The only issue was that he felt inclined to tell every soul his story and at every hour of the day as well. 'I fought the cancer and I beat it, but it came back', blah blah blah. He obviously didn't say 'blah blah blah' but wallowing in my self-pity and rage that's all I could hear after the fifth time I heard that story. In my defence he did keep me up in the middle of the night telling an old man about his diagnosis. But it doesn't excuse how rude I was about him.

And I hope he's alive now and he reads this, and he knows I'm talking about him (hint: you're annoying).

I want to say I'm sorry. You were super annoying, but like me, it may have come from a place you don't often go to. I won't promise not to be rude to anyone else − I'm still working on my own issues − but I'm truly sorry for what I said about you.

CHEZ MOI

Eventually I got moved to my own room on the ward. En-suite, my own TV, butler service etc (one of those is a fat lie). I had two tables, one over the bed and one against the wall, opposite to the head of the bed. Which meant I could put the supplied TV facing me sat in bed. It was small but crucially had terrestrial TV channels so I could watch crap at any hour of the day.

Doesn't sound so bad does it?

It wasn't really and I'm grateful to have had my own space to rage at people and vomit in. It however quickly became a prison for me, and I learned about every inch of that room. As the minutes became hours I would sit there on my own staring at the walls and ceiling. I couldn't really sit and look out of the window from my position on the bed, meaning weather and external temperature became like religion to me; there – important – but not for me.

I had big beef with all the staff about closing my room door – yes, I am that petty and yes, I need you to know about it. My room was directly opposite the nurse's station and entrance to the ward, so if the door was open, I would hear pretty much every word of pretty much every conversation. At one a.m. when my eyes wouldn't stay open, I would hear 'U alrigh Yvonne? U on nights agen eh?' So annoying...

Towards the end of my stay a member of staff took pity on me and put a 'Please close the door' sign on the outside of my door. All this did was make me look like a prick and gave nurses an excuse to ignore me because I was 'closed to the public'.

Note to self – don't rock the boat.

HAVE YOU LOCKED IN THE PRISONER?

You'd think someone that works in a hospital would be polite as they could be with the staff? You'd think they'd display some of the empathy they claim to use at work every day? Well, you'd think wrong. My room was not a sea of tranquillity, if you pissed me off then I'd tell you about it. I argued with nurses and other staff. Not especially proud but I wasn't really myself.

I guess I probably should have spared the staff looking after me some of my pig-headed-ness; normally I'm overly polite. I get anxious if a houseguest hasn't been offered a hot drink within two minutes of stepping through the door.

But therein lies the problem – I wasn't in my house. I wasn't in control. I couldn't lock my door. Sure, people knocked, but there wasn't a damn thing I could do to stop them coming in. Somehow, my door always being open (or unlocked at least) made me feel the opposite of sociable – I felt alone. Because as sure as people wandered in through that door, it wasn't long until they walked out again. It reminds me of one of my favourite Police lyrics: 'In this desert that I call my soul, I always play the starring role'. It's a beautiful sentiment, if roughly shoe-horned to my situation.

You Won't Believe this Shit

The toilet in my room became a kind of weird, satanic shrine. No, it wasn't full of pictures of Mark Hoffman, it was a place I was scared of using but still held great import over me. I had terrible constipation, probably because of the meds but more likely I offended the wrong people in management...

Most people think of being constipated as a very transient thing that disappears by morning. What a lot of people may not realise is that when you need to go the toilet and you can't, you experience severe abdominal pain and nausea.

I was so far gone I needed an enema a couple of times; for those that have had one before, skip forward – you don't need to be reminded.

***

For those yet to experience an enema, imagine rolling around on the bed in pain like your internal organs are on fire. Then imagine someone's shoved a wine cork up your backside and instructed your body to vomit when someone asks you how they can help.

Without spoiling your day any further I'll sum this all up: 1) Enema goes up anus. 2) Patient is instructed to wait at least fifteen minutes for enema to work (longer the better). 3) Patient rolls around bed shouting and swearing at people. 4) After five minutes patient ignores advice and runs to toilet. 5)

Patient's problems go down the drain (the best humour is toilet-humour).

An Apple a Day Keeps the Cancer Away

People joke about the quality of hospital food and how it probably makes you feel worse than when you first arrived in hospital. People have tried all sorts of things to help improve it, and by people, I mean people like Jamie Oliver (probably need a fact-check here but I'm sure I've seen him on TV in hospital – if not he should be!)

If I could devote a whole book to it I would; every day, three times a day for about three months I would order food, make the wrong decision, swear a lot and then do it all again the next day.

I'm not going to list the menu or tell you which dishes in particular made me want to throw up. There isn't enough digital ink in my laptop...

The problem is that the powers that be have decided that if you're in hospital, then the food offered has to be nutritionally balanced or whatever. They offered me a choice of soup (disgusting), sandwich (disgustinger) or 'hot meal' involving lasagne/pasta/mashed potato etc (disgustingest).

I know I come across as ungrateful – I know. I don't really want to insult the people in the hospital kitchens directly; they had probably hundreds of poor souls to feed, en-masse and with a limited budget. I guess it stresses how important food was to me and to patients in general. You don't think about it until you're in that position yourself, I guess.

I'm white, with an ethnic background. 'Here we go,' I hear you say. Anyway, ethnic food growing up, ethnic name, issues with my name pronounced on the school register etc. I think I'm probably being a massive racist here, but they only made 'white food' in hospital. Sweet and Sour Chicken made with no seasoning and nothing sweet or sour does not give you 'ethnic food', just an imitation of it. I'm not going to divulge the foods in question (except the one I just did) because I'm already being rude.

If you're a white, indigenous British person then you're probably offended that I'm highlighting your diet as dog food. If you're not a white, indigenous British person, you might still be offended. I'll live. As long as I don't have to live on hospital food until I die.

They did a similar thing in schools; I remember burger and chips and food that made you feel better about being in a terrible f**king place. When my son goes to school, he'll be offered either quinoa or hummus to go with his vegan burger.

Since leaving hospital I've made a list of foods I miss and slowly I've been ticking them off – stuff like onion rings or mac 'n' cheese. Like an American man's bucket list but hopefully less fatal at the end.

THE PILL POPPER

Meds. Meds meds meds. Medications. Poisons. Whatever you call them, I've had them all. Apart from the obvious horrible chemotherapy drugs which I'll cover later, they gave me loads of different medications to help control my nausea. You name it, I've popped it.

From the second I woke up after my operation I felt sick. I vomited for the first time whilst still reeling from the anaesthetic drugs, little did I know, it would be the first of many to come – because it was horrific. A bit like your First Time (I've capitalised it for all the adults in the room), it's rubbish to start with and doesn't get any better for a while.

As you can imagine I don't quite remember what happened, I didn't have my wife as my official Chronicler in Theatre Recovery, so God knows what I said or did... I remember asking the anaesthetic doctor before the operation to give me loads of anti-sickness drugs. Obviously, I predicted how bad I'd feel from that point onwards.

So yes, the meds. Without banging on too much, I then began the long process of 'managing my nausea' by trying every pill in the book. I had tablets, intra-venous drugs, drugs that are injected under my skin, patches on my arm, patches on my neck and combinations of each of them.

I recall at one point having a couple of tablets, a patch of whatever on my neck and a needle placed under the skin on my arm attached to a machine that drip fed me drugs over twenty-four hours. Not into my veins like most drugs, but under my skin. I had that stupid machine attached to me like a bad smell, making that stupid noise and constantly beeping if the battery was running out. I hated that machine like I hated people who drive Harley Davidsons early in the morning.

There was however, one thing that united all the meds; they didn't bloody work. I recall hearing the term 'guinea pig' when describing my treatment options. The doctors didn't know what to do with my nausea. It was a case of 'try this, try that. Errr, let's see if this combination works?' The other ball-ache was that you had to wait a few days before trying another cocktail of medications. So, I had to try a few different combinations to see if they worked. Which they never did. 'Give it a few days, let's see if it works.' Got bored of that phrase fairly early on...

I became an experiment, no-one knew if any medication would work on me, it became the hot topic in almost every conversation with my medical team. Towards the end of my stay my doctors had to apply to the health authority for permission to give me certain drugs (money issues essentially). They even applied for a cannabis-derived drug which seemed to ruffle a few feathers. Didn't work. Sent it back after a couple of days. And no, I didn't try to sell any. Although I bet no-one would have suspected me...

***

There was one drug which worked on me. Sort of. Because I had so many drugs into my veins, it was decided for me to have a longer-term line inserted which goes up into my bigger vessels coming out of my heart. This meant I didn't have to keep getting pricked with needles every time I needed a blood test or have certain medications. Putting it mildly you don't put those lines in well patients....

Back to the meds (again). There was one drug, designed for anti-sickness but very much for use as a short-lived 'when I feel sick' kind of remedy. It's called Cyclizine and it only helped when given into the vein. I had it in tablet form and the under-skin-preparation, but they did nothing. Essentially when given by vein this medication gives you a head-rush. My heart rate would settle, I'd calm down and forget about my exhausting nausea. In the words of Travis Scott, I was the highest in the room, by a long way.

The catch? It would only last ten to fifteen minutes and then I'd sink back into my bed-prison, back into the feeling that I believed would never go away. I won't mince words, it's the kind of drug wrong-uns request when they get admitted for an alcohol overdose or something they shouldn't have done. And I was addicted.

Not in the traditional sense, my last dose was my last dose and I weaned myself off it without any fuss. I was addicted at the time because it became the only thing that made me feel any better. I was addicted to the feeling that I didn't need to be nauseous. It became a – very – temporary relief, a couple of times a day.

Imagine being on the deck of a ferry in rough seas. Now imagine you can freeze the sea and the boat – but only for ten minutes at a time. After which, the torture continues.

I'm fairly sure people thought I was a wrong-un, but I just didn't care. I'm better now and I don't need anti-sickness meds, and to be honest I don't need that feeling anymore either. I was a victim/slave/guinea pig to those treatments and one of my major achievements is no longer needing them.

WHAT'S THE ALTERNATIVE DOC? REALLY???

Alternative therapies. You know; Reflexology, Aromatherapy or Meditation to name a few. Whether you believe in them or not they're here to stay and to some they come with their own Old and New Testament. In hospital I had loads of stuff to try and alleviate my nausea or attempt to magic my cancer away. I had magic healing bands, magic smelly fragrances, magic meditation lessons etc etc.

The one thing that really helped were these amazing foot rubs. I'm not a massage-seeking, metrosexual kinda guy but if I recommend anything, it's having a nice lady with dreadlocks rub scented oil into your feet. I think it's called Reflexology but we both know I didn't give a damn at the time.

I'm going to throw my hat in the ring and say that Alternative therapies are a load of horseshit designed to satisfy the stupid, stupider and stupidest. There are lots of desperate people that pin a lot of hope on scented candles curing their fungal toe infection and I can't help sighing every time someone tells me something like that. I can't help it. And I have a fair amount of actual, personal experience, unlike a lot of non-believers.

Now you may hear a faint note of dripping sarcasm in my account, and I have more than a few stories about foreign parents who stop medications for their children, move to another country to try and shrink their tumour with daily doses of turmeric. Then come crawling back to the NHS with a look of total, bewildered incredulity on their faces, 'I don't understand Doctor, we were told if she eats an apple a day, she'll never have to see another doctor?'

But then, almost everyone, me included, has that friend of a friend who waved tea-tree oil under their nose every day for a week and their eczema mysteriously vanished. There are multiple reports of people praying and their cancer melting away overnight. Acupuncture actually has a shred of evidence saying that it might help people in some way (I've had it in the past, it definitely did not help me in any way).

Hold on though. That's not entirely what I believe anymore. I have relaxed my views towards Alternative therapies recently, not because I've found a miracle cure for cancer in some old coffee granules, but because I now genuinely believe that there are people out there that believe rubbing your feet can get rid of your crippling asthma. I believe that they believe.

So. In summary. Because I'm a doctor and not a pure scientist, I have to try and present a balanced view of Alternative therapies and their place in this world. I owe this to my patients and their families.

And my balanced view is that it's absolute crap and dangerous should you forgo Western Medicine in order to rely on it. If my son stopped taking an inhaler and puffed on a turnip instead, I think I'd hand myself into the nearest police station or hang myself from the ceiling.

However, for some people where there isn't a satisfactory cure, or people like me that were frankly desperate to try something – then I believe you should go ahead, knock yourself out, go crazy. Just don't offer me a turmeric smoothie anytime soon.

Is Anyone Listening?

Maybe this isn't the right format to discuss religion and its role in my recovery. But thinking about Alternative therapies and people praying for mercy from the heavens above must have set something celestial off in my brain. Or what's left of it.

I don't believe in a higher power, nor do I believe in chewing someone's ear off to get your views across. I don't believe in agnosticism/vegetarianism (same thing?). I don't believe that someone did this to me. I don't believe anyone prayed for this to happen to me either.

I do believe however that it's not what happens to you, rather the way you deal with it that makes the difference. Maybe that's ordained by a higher power, maybe it isn't. It doesn't make a difference to me because what's done is done and its no-one's fault. No-one's.

I think I may have prayed to God at some point. Prayed for a reversal of my fortunes whilst not actually believing in who I was supposed to be praying to. It's like that scene in films where the protagonist (or hero, I'm not fussed how you picture me) drops to their knees and prays for a magic sword or something to be able to save the world with.

Only I prayed not to be sick anymore. Not for the health and happiness of my family but for my own stupid, selfish self.

Maybe that's why no-one answered, and why I didn't get my pony either.

THE CHRISTMAS TURKEY

I was allowed to go out of hospital on Christmas Day. On a home-leave basis. I woke up in hospital, I was wheeled into a car and then transported to my sofa in the flat my wife and I were renting at the time. I opened presents, had lunch and then a few hours later when I ran out of steam, I was dumped back in my hospital bed, little TV on, fell asleep alone. I might have cried in the dark, can't remember. Not my favourite Christmas Day ever.

You may think I was resentful at being abandoned back in hospital, I'm not, I was only allowed out on the provision that I eventually returned.

My family (direct and extended) were amazing, they made a full Christmas Dinner, there were presents and merriment. Jesus, I'm not sure I've ever used the word 'merriment' before. Anyhow, they sat me down with my paper crown, shit film in the background and a plate of food. I couldn't eat much at that point, but I remember enjoying what I could manage. There are some God-awful pictures of me taken that day which will hopefully never surface. I probably looked miserable in them, but it goes down as a happy day in my memory. That's what Christmas is for I guess, happiness through family.

My Christmas present from my wife was a new Apple Watch, designed to force me to acknowledge calls and texts from my wrist whilst in hospital. It made perfect sense because when I lay down in my hospital bed my phone was placed on the bedside table just above and behind my right side. It was an absolute pain to reach up and grab it, so I generally left it if I heard a phone call or text. With the new watch, I had no excuse but to acknowledge when someone tried to contact me. Masterstroke. An expensive masterstroke but a solution to a problem none the less.

Cancer - A Truly Natural Diet

My weight was an issue for the doctors. Nausea + vomiting + hospital food = missed meals. I couldn't even stomach my wife's cooking that she brought in (she's a good cook as well). My parents brought in a McDonalds burger meal for us all to share at one point – other evil multi-national restaurant chains are available.

My mother hates stuff like that as well so a good effort from her. I made a dent, but I usually demolish the whole meal. I must have looked like a sad little puppy when they cleared away an unfinished burger and milkshake. There was even a damn milkshake and I couldn't finish it... Other evil multi-national restaurant chain milkshakes are available.

The lack of eating was an issue, my weight dropped by around ten kilos which, I can assure you, was not the result of a new Keto diet or whatever. The team tried their best, I had a lovely nutritionist who provided these damn awful milkshakes for me. They're meant to be 'flavoured' nutrient/calorie-rich shakes that you can drink multiple times a day, to supplement your diet and provide you with the calories you're desperately missing.

For the drinkers, have you ever had a 'Dirty Pint'? It's a horrible drink you get on your birthday if you haven't been kind to your friends; everyone tips a bit of their drink into an empty pint glass. If you haven't been kind to the bar man then they'll helpfully add some milk and vodka to the glass, just to make sure it curdles. When the drink's ready you then have to drink it in one, curdled milk included.

Sounds disgusting doesn't it? Now imagine drinking something just as disgusting, but every day, after/before each meal, three times a day. Now picture eager faces smiling at you, willing you to drink even though they know how bad it is. I know now how anorexics feel, like its feeding-time at the petting zoo.

Despite the milkshakes, my weight continued to fall. One day I was informed if I didn't reverse my weight loss then I would have to get a RIG, or Radiologically Inserted Gastrostomy. It's basically a tube inserted directly into the stomach with a spout on the surface of the skin that they can use to pump artificial food into the stomach. Essentially a feeding tube that bypasses the mouth and throat and avoids any nausea. Not permanent but most likely an end to my stomach-modelling aspirations.

I thought about it and talked it over with my family. The medical team wanted it because they were worried about my weight and wanted me to recover faster. My family didn't want it because it's disfiguring and a definite step back in my treatment. I've simplified both cases, but it came to a head when I was next weighed. My weight had fallen below the magic line and it was decision-time.

So, I decided. I told the medical team, 'yeh go for it, whatever. Just wait till my wife gets here'. I lacked the nerve and because I'm a useless male, it seemed I lacked the ability to consent to anything as well.

As it turns out I made the right decision in making no decision and waiting for my wife to come. She flipped out when I told her, and she demanded that someone weighed me there and then. Turns out I hadn't lost as much weight as we thought; a member of staff had incorrectly recorded my weight previously and set everyone off down the wrong road.

Being threatened with a stomach tube obviously did the trick because my weight slowly increased, and I never heard the term 'RIG' again.

I'M FINALLY FREE - OH WAIT.

They let me go home in mid-January. My discharge was such an anti-climax, considering I'd been there for so damn long, I think I expected more. I didn't deserve more, there isn't some sort of NHS loyalty card; the worse you feel the more discount you get at Costa. There's a morbid thought for you...

Maybe the anti-climax was just as well, I'm not sure a red carpet and brass band would have made me feel any better. I don't actually remember much; I held my boy close of course – that was my only real aspiration for the day. The rest is a blur, can't remember what I had to eat or even who was there.

You hear people who have been away for a while (prison or a gap year) talk about their memories of returning home. Usually, some bullshit about having a hot bath or making sweet love to their partner. I stumbled through the door, no doubt propped up by my family, probably saying that I felt sick or tired or something that everyone had already heard. Didn't belong in the land of the living and didn't belong in the land of the dead either. I felt like a weird uncle returning to the family fold after serving time for the 'incident'.

My discharge was pre-planned of course – it wasn't decided in a vision at the bottom of my Rice Krispies. The next stage of my recovery was to go home, sit and wait for my chemotherapy to start; roughly six weeks after my radiotherapy finished.

At last! Something as an outpatient! I don't have to fall asleep alone or wait until eight or nine pm when the good TV starts!

I was convinced as soon as I woke up in my own bed I'd be back to my normal self, fighting fit and going back to work the following week – I'd need a rest after all.

***

Yeah right. I woke up the following day in my own clothes but a trembling shadow of myself. I couldn't walk in a straight line, speak on the phone properly or drive my own damn car. I was so far away from going back to work I should have sent a postcard.

Discharge was simply the next phase in my ordeal.

Inwardly, I had a big issue with routine, or lack of it. I tried not to show it but in hospital the nurse came into my room around the same time in the morning. Crap daytime TV started at the same time every morning. Lunch was at twelve, dinner at five, you get the idea.

I had been institutionalised purely by spending so long away from home. Like the poor old man who left prison in The Shawshank Redemption (although it didn't end the same way).

My symptoms were still around to deal with, so life wasn't exactly how it used to be. I didn't have any bottles to pee into at night, I had to get up and go to the bathroom. The indignity!

I guess I craved a sense of normality through my old routine (I've been told by friends and enemies alike that I'm neurotic, maybe it was an observation and not an insult), I wanted to walk and talk normally, I wanted people to see me as a pair of comfortable shoes – back to when I was in a comfortable place. Instead, I looked like Quasimodo with both feet tied together.

IKEA

Not everything about my condition was doom and gloom; some unique opportunities presented themselves to me whilst I was supposed to be miserable and disabled. Opportunities for mischief that would never have the light of day if not for my cancer.

My favourite: one summer's day I tagged along to our nearest IKEA with my wife and mother-in-law. We may have been buying a new wardrobe, or a treehouse, or possibly a loft conversion – you never really know with IKEA and I can't remember anyway.

I was being pushed around in the wheelchair the NHS had provided for me when I left hospital. Physically I could walk but as everyone knows, the walk around the IKEA shop floor is about a hundred miles long and so I just wasn't up to the task at that point. I've since been back to IKEA and walked around on my own two feet, but my only motivation was at the end of the Swedish ultra-marathon, I would get at least three hotdogs, covered in ketchup, mustard and regret.

Back to my first furniture foray: there we were, strolling through a relatively quiet week-day IKEA, me, my wife and her mother. Now I wouldn't describe myself as particularly metrosexual, or particularly bothered about spending my time shopping in general. At the same time, I'm not Neanderthal in my view towards retail therapy, I'll do it when it's necessary. But going around IKEA with my wife and her enabler, sorry, her mother – is possibly the most boring and frustrating thing a man – no, a human – can be asked to do.

'Will this look good in the bathroom?' No chance to reply, 'No I've changed my mind, it's too white, I don't like it anymore.'

Okay...

'Do we need more houseplants?'

'No, we don't.'

'Ok, I'll just go back and quickly pick a few up.'

Moments later she returns with eight pots balancing on various limbs and of course, 'Ooh I've got some more candles.'

Of course you do...

So now I'm starting to ruminate about how many Swedish meatballs I would need to eat to kill myself whilst being pushed around in my wheelchair. Then I start to moan to my jailers about being bored, Disabled Rights and how inhumanely I was being treated but to no avail...

Time to take matters into my own hands:

'HELP! THEY'RE HURTING ME!!!'

Now, obviously nobody was harming me, but the entirety of IKEA Manchester's shoppers didn't know that. My captors both shot me a look of death, went bright red and begged me to shut up but not before they began to nervously wrap up their previously leisurely IKEA trip.

I've never felt so proud of myself in that moment and at the same time, disappointed in the pathetic response from the Manchester public to a potential abuse scandal of an individual in a wheelchair. Oh well, I got what I needed from that day.

That wheelchair is long gone now and so is the chance to replicate my favourite ever trip to IKEA. The err, 'strong feelings', experienced by my wife and her mother – they remain.

FOR DESSERT, OUR FINEST CHEMOTHERAPY MONSIEUR

My chemotherapy started as planned. There wasn't a red carpet or tons of paparazzi waiting at the treatment centre for me. Or maybe they were at the back entrance... In any case my expectations were warped.

For some reason I thought I would be put into a deep sleep like Sleeping Beauty (dress optional). Someone would hook me up to a drip and then hours later I'd wake up and Beyoncé would be standing over me, pulling away from a kiss. The chemotherapy would be finished, and everyone would be smiling. Then, my hair dropped off my head and all of Beyoncé's teeth fell out. I vomit a rainbow and then – wait a second - maybe that was a dream...

In reality, bits of that account are true.

No – wait - it's all rubbish...

Back to reality.

***

I got there, sat on a bed, waited for the nurse, let them put a cannula (allows you to inject drugs into the veins) in my arm, waited for a bit, started the chemotherapy drip, waited for it to finish, went to the toilet because all the drips make you want to wee every ten minutes, started the next dose of chemotherapy, waited some more, had some oral tablets, finished the bag of chemotherapy and then finally waited for the last 'flush' bag to finish. Oh no wait, I forgot that once the last bag finished, I had to sit and wait for the nurse to come and disconnect me and remove the cannula from my arm. Then, and only then, could I go.

***

Phew... I was probably there from eight or nine a.m. till the evening. Some people came in for chemotherapy and left a few hours later. I think they were supposed to come every day for a bit, but my treatment was to have a day of chemotherapy every six weeks until I'd had six rounds of it. To give my body time to recover in-between doses.

I felt remarkably well after my doses. I mean, I generally felt like crap heated through but I'm not sure the chemotherapy drugs did anything to make me feel worse than I already did. I felt tired, nauseous and wobbly (technical term) before and after the chemotherapy. I ended up lying to myself and my family and using the treatment as an excuse 'oh, I must be tired from the chemotherapy'. But I felt better at the end of the chemotherapy than I did at the beginning (the dose effect was supposed to be cumulative – as in any side-effects were supposed to appear later on).

My facial hair remained untouched (small respite for my modelling career) and the hair on top of my head was beginning to grow back. This added to the theory me and my wife had that medications simply don't touch me, chemotherapy included.

Stick or Twist

I had a big decision to make at this point. I'd had three cycles of chemotherapy before I started to think enough was enough. Like an abusive spouse, I couldn't seem to let go of something I knew was potentially damaging me. However, unlike an abusive spouse, the chemotherapy was supposed to be prolonging my life. Although I seemed to be getting better overall, there are some nasty long-term effects from chemotherapy that I was eager to avoid. Like infertility or an increased risk of future cancer.

Without getting too technical, my dilemma with the treatment was that there isn't much evidence that my tumour responds to the type of chemotherapy I was being given. My cancer is a rare beast that usually affects children, not adults. Therefore, there isn't much scientific research into what treatments work, and which don't for me.

Chemotherapy is not a nice thing. Broadly speaking, its poison. In my opinion, it's the most ironic thing a doctor can give to a cancer patient – give someone a poison in order to help get rid of a poison. Alanis Morissette would be turning in her grave hearing this, still looking for a knife amidst all the spoons.

And therein lay my dilemma, do I finish all six cycles of chemotherapy and potentially leave my body riddled with permanent side effects? Remember that there's a lack of evidence to show the drugs affect my tumour at all.

Or, do I stop early and stem the tide of chemotherapy effects, but put myself at risk of the cancer being under-treated?

What would you do?

***

I spent what felt like an age asking people around me what would they do? Stick or twist? Confucius once claimed, 'The man who asks a question is a fool for a minute, the man who does not ask is a fool for life.' So, I asked as many people as I could for advice. When I asked, a lot of the time I would get the same answer, 'it depends on you, how you feel.'

Some people said do this, some people said do that. This was the first big decision I was being asked to make in a long time. There wasn't really a decision to make at the beginning of the treatment; lie there and we'll remove this tumour, lie there and we'll fry your internal organs with this radiotherapy, lie there and take these pills and see how you feel.

Now, I was faced with a choice. I'm a married man with a child; I emphatically hate being given choices. I want my wife to decide stuff like this for me, I know she'll make the right decision and we'll all live happily ever after. Only she couldn't decide for me – maybe she wanted to kill me off and replace me with Jason Momoa (I think I'd replace her with Jason Momoa) but maybe she was just relieved that she didn't have to make the decision herself. And no-one, even me, expected her to do that. I would have asked my son but I'm fairly certain at that point he would have just told me to stop being 'naughty' and then run off screaming.

So. I decided. I stopped my chemotherapy after four cycles out of six. My doctor told me he was happy that I got to four cycles and the greatest effect was from the first couple of rounds. That made me feel better, although there was a nagging voice in my ear telling me I may have just signed my own death warrant.

Why did I do it? I think maybe I was sick of being a patient; I couldn't leave the country whilst on chemotherapy, couldn't go to work, couldn't drive etc. Although, I've said before, I wasn't convinced the chemotherapy was contributing to any side-effects, I wasn't convinced I was getting any sicker on the drugs.

I wasn't convinced but I still talked myself into the decision. I would say asking my loved ones gave a mixed response; most decisions on treatment like this are a question of stopping something you know might be working, you just can't tolerate the side effects. My choice was different and even now, faced with the same dilemma, I would struggle.

Writing this today I'm not regretting anything, and if my cancer comes back it may not be because I stopped the chemotherapy, it may be just plain bad luck. There's no magic blood test that will tell you how much cancer is left in your body or when it'll start to grow back and ruin your day. I have serial MRI scans of my head now, to see if anything comes back and so far, so good.

STEPPING ONTO THE PROPERTY LADDER

I live with my wife and son in an amazing three bed semi in a lovely area. Before they found a whacking great tumour in my head, my wife and I had been on countless house viewings in the south of Manchester. We'd actually been waiting in a long and boring chain at the time of my diagnosis (another story, another time) and we were forced to complete the purchase whilst I was sat in my hospital bed.

It went that way because some people up the chain didn't want to wait a few days while they went on holiday around Christmas, and so they threatened to pull out and ruin the whole thing. This forced the people ahead of us to push for completion as well. My wife tried in vain to stall them, at least until I could walk out of my hospital room unaided, but no dice.

I remember barely being able to read my phone and having to call the bank to transfer thousands of pounds to our solicitor's accounts. I could barely speak, maybe a bit like the Godfather, 'You come to me on the day of my daughter's wedding???'

I'd just like to say to those people that put us in that position – f**k you.

F**k you and everything about you for being so selfish. You were told about me in no uncertain terms, you chose not to care about anyone but yourself. I don't know your names, but I hope your new house burns down with you in it.

You Know Who You Are

My wife told me that whilst in hospital, she had a lot of back and forth with the estate agents regarding the house sale. I won't name names, but a certain estate agent said something to my wife that I hope they sincerely regret.

Whilst I was recovering from my surgery, trying to decide whether or not to buy the house, the estate agent pressured my wife to complete the sale. They did this by attempting to guilt-trip her and told her that the family moving from our future house were all packed up and didn't want to spend Christmas surrounded by moving boxes.

You can imagine the answer my wife gave to that comment... You can imagine how anyone would react to that whilst their spouse was half-way between life and death in a cancer hospital. I don't know if that nugget of stupidity came from the vendors themselves or just the idiot estate agent but whoever came up with that, I hope you realise what you've said. I hope you take it to the grave, because I will.

WHY BOTHER?

'Why bother' I hear you ask. 'Why not wait for another house', 'why not wait until you're better?' Well, after many sleepless nights those questions became easier to answer and trust me, everyone asked me the same questions.

I pushed for us to sign for the house because I wanted my wife and child to live in a nice house in a nice area, near nice schools and not too far from either set of grandparents. It was the best house we'd seen in our budget and we had been so keen to move in before I was taken ill. It would have been like taking a child's Christmas presents away, we were so excited about moving in we'd picked out and designed where the furniture would be.

The real reason I wanted my family in that home was that I was scared. I was terrified that I was going to die and that my family would still be renting a flat somewhere. Bear in mind my wife is a doctor, an intelligent woman and entirely sensible – I still felt like I would leave them with nothing. Now I know that was totally stupid, if I died my wife probably wouldn't appreciate having a big mortgage and a toddler to look after on her own but I'm sure you're aware by now, I wasn't thinking straight.

So, I signed. Out of fear. We made the right decision in the end, but there's no denying it should have been made in a more comfortable place.

What Am I?

Here's a thought: Am I disabled? Am I a disabled person? Am I a Disabled Doctor©®™

I walk and talk funny, no hiding it. But am I disabled? By the letter of the law, I am classified as a disabled person and I still use my Blue Badge in the car (flipping life saver).

But I don't feel like I am. I mean, I am different to other people. Not fat-kid-at-school-with-dirty-clothes-and-a-lisp different but, you know, different. I've been rude about people that are different before, never to intentionally hurt but mainly for cheap laughs.

Now I'm wondering if I'm the subject of a cheap laugh somewhere. Not that I don't probably deserve it and not that

I'm particularly offended, I have skin like a rhinoceros. I think I'm more bothered if people who might potentially rely on me, think differently about me when they see me stagger about. I'm talking about parents of children in hospital really. I'm not too fussed if the person in McDonalds cleaning the tables has a double look at me - other evil multi-national restaurant chain tables are available to clean by the way.

But still, in my own head, my perception of myself has changed. I no longer see Gaston in the mirror (Google it, just assume I'm not exaggerating). At the time of writing, I've regained my gut; my muscle mass generally is at 'timid kitten' level and my hair is thin and still filling out. I don't want to see a tiny violin being played for me and I know some people with my cancer haven't lived to the point where their abdomen slowly expands with onion rings and mac 'n' cheese.

I guess I just don't see the man I was anymore. And as flawed as he was, he was much further away from death than I am. But he was a bit of a Chubby Puppy, can't dispute that.

Ma Team

My parents were understandably worried about me, my father in particular. I don't think my mother was doing her impression of the Ice Queen from Narnia, far from it. I just felt that it affected my father more. He hasn't had cancer and I hope he never does but I could tell from his words and actions that he was upset about me.

They were there at the beginning and at every major waypoint on my journey. They visited me, brought me food, listened to my seemingly endless rants and spoke to me about normal life – which I appreciated.

There's a lot I could, and probably should, say about my parents and their role in my recovery. A lot of people in that hospital may not have parents still with us, or parents that give a damn. I love my parents and one day I'll repay them for what they've done for me. The amount of text I've devoted to them here doesn't convey the significance they hold in my life. Many people say they love their parents, I trust my parents with my life.

My brother has to have a mention here, for completeness of course. He lives in Paris and so couldn't be here all the time, he has a life and girlfriend over there, but he was never far away if I needed him. He was worried about me, and maybe the distance made it worse, I don't know. My brother is an asshole (other, more positive but incorrect opinions are available) and I love him in an entirely different way to my wife or parents, but I love him all the same.

This section has to include a word about my mother-in-law; she was there from the beginning helping me whilst in hospital and she was there with my wife, helping to look after my son. She witnessed me being an asshole (infectious word, you should try it) towards my wife and talked with me about how shitty everything was. She helped keep me afloat in this sea of misery and I'll always be eternally grateful. Just keep that Demon Dog away from me (she knows what I'm on about).

Ma Wife

At this stage in the story, I've mentioned my wife thirty-eight times. That's a rubbish return on the number of times I talk about her in real life. It's a rubbish return on the amount of time in the day I spend thinking about her. This is a rubbish way to pay tribute to her as well, if I could devote ten thousand words to how much I love her I would – it might not be worthy of Keats or Shakespeare but they're dead now so it's my time to shine.

My wife is one of the main reasons I wake up every morning in this Never-Ending Story of Melancholy, one of the main reasons I didn't try and jump off the roof whilst in hospital, one of the main reasons I want to get back to work and provide for her and my son. If a bus has to hit one of us, I hope it's me. Just not a very big bus, you know?

There seems to be an infinite list of superlatives to describe your spouse. An endless list of comparisons and exaggerations (shall I compare thee to a summer's McFlurry?)

that mean something in the moment and then fade away into the sands of time.

My description of my wife is that I just can't live without her, in a literal and Shakespearean sense. She is my friend, wife and my crutch, all at the same time.

My wife is the one person I'm worried about reading this. Maybe because she's been right next to me throughout all of it. She's so close that I'm worried our stories are intertwined and parallel at the same time. Is there a sunnier, more positive version of events in her head and in reality? Is my version of events not dark enough? Are my thoughts and feelings accurate? Does she deserve to have to experience my thoughts and feelings?

Or maybe I don't want her to have to relive any of this. After all, she knows what's happened. We've shared the highs and lows, we've both cried together and we've both talked things into the ground. Should she go through all of this again? I'm not sure she should. Like that rollercoaster ride that made you sick when you were younger; why the hell would you ride it again?

At the point where I asked my family to read this memoir to gauge its quality/readability I offered to show my wife. She refused and I don't blame her. 'Too soon' I think she said. Fair enough. Suits me for now.

MA BOY

I've glossed over my son up to this point. I haven't written about him enough, I know. He was and still is the best thing I've done or could have hoped to have done. At the point when I first went into hospital, he was almost eighteen months old but couldn't yet walk properly (late walker but early monster).

I had to watch videos of him on my phone learning to walk around our flat, whilst I was laid on my hospital bed. The boy could soon walk better than his father and just thinking about him made me weep like a teenage girl at a Justin Bieber concert. Or maybe it was just the meds.

Point blank I refused to have my son visit me whilst on the ward. I told my family it was because I didn't want him to catch any of these 'NHS superbugs', or that in my immuno-compromised (weakened immune system) state, I was a danger to him and myself. True facts but not the whole story.

My wife showed me her notebook where she recorded all of the significant events since I first fell ill. She wrote that I saw my son in a cafè in the atrium of the first hospital I stayed in. I don't remember that at all. Damn.

I do remember however, the following month (in the second hospital) seeing him in another hospital cafè. I remember it because I was sat in my wheelchair and he was staggering about me with my family looking on. I remember lifting him (or being handed him) and holding him in my arms. I remember breaking down and crying like a baby. My son wasn't crying like a baby, ironically, he was being the grown-up one. I'm crying right now typing this, I don't think anything or anyone else in my life has made me both as elated and deflated at the same time.

The truth was, despite the validity of my other excuses, I was petrified of him seeing me in a hospital bed. I was petrified of him seeing me upset. I was petrified of him seeing me in pyjamas in the middle of the day. But most of all I was petrified of him not recognising me as his father.

One of my biggest regrets of being in hospital and being away from home for so long was how my wife had to look after our son day and night. She got him out of bed, took him to nursery, fed him, bathed him, changed him, put him to bed, listened to his cries and visited me in hospital every chance she could. Now, when I say regret; I knew he was in the best possible hands. I knew he was loved and that everything was under control.

Yet I felt like I was abandoning him, letting him down, even though I could hardly teleport to his side from my hospital bed. I had to recover; I knew that. But I felt like an absent father, and it made me respect my wife even more for what she did. I love both of you.

WHEN WILL IT ALL BE OVER?

Remission. As in remission from cancer, defined as the signs and symptoms of your cancer being reduced or gone, and in either a partial or complete form. There are different criteria considered such as the amount of tumour being removed or measured, length of time with no discernible disease or even a noticeable reduction in observable signs or symptoms.

This concept became my own, personal Mount Everest. Attainable; yet really flipping far away.

At the time of writing this bit, I asked my Oncologist if I was in remission or not? Now before I reveal his answer, I challenge you to Google 'cancer remission definition' and see if you can come to a concrete consensus about when or how my situation could be termed 'in remission'.

Not straightforward is it?

And that determined the answer my doctor gave me; essentially 'not yet, maybe after a few years without cancer, it depends'.

For someone who gets cold sweats thinking about puzzles with one missing piece, this level of anti-OCD just didn't ring my bell. However, at the point of asking the question, I was only about a year cancer-free and so I knew there was still time to revisit the subject. I simply nodded and moved on.

***

Therein lies my internal strife: I was struggling towards remission, but my doctor/family were setting my sights earth-bound, like getting back to work or being able to drive again. My own expectations were wildly high and yet I didn't really communicate my feelings at the time. Any talk of remission became yesterday's news.

I didn't want it to be like that. I didn't want to prepare emotionally for the cancer to come back. I didn't want to be looking over my shoulder for the rest of my life. Call me an egotistical maniac but I wanted my illness to be a one-time thing, followed by an epic montage of my recovery whilst achieving all of Heracles' Twelve Labours.

And that's why the notion of 'remission' has endured as a fixed point in my mental model of how my life should be. There doesn't currently seem to be much hiding behind it at the end of the tunnel, no 'have five children', no 'become a philanthropist' or even 'buy a house with a sex dungeon'.

I have a vision of a fifty-year old me wearing a T-shirt brandishing the phrase, 'Straight Outta Remission' and reminiscing about a time when I carried airplane sick bags in my coat pocket, just in case I decided not to vomit on a stranger's shoes.

I just want to live.

I just don't want to die and beforehand be reminded of it at regular intervals before I do go.

I just want to live.

Is that so much to ask?

If You don't Laugh, You'll cry

I'm translating this mental diarrhoea into text at this point, at the expense of logical story progression and comic appeal, simply because I can and also because this part of the memoir seems like a good place to write about serious stuff. Well, the whole thing is supposed to be untangling sombre subjects, but I've always held the belief that it doesn't matter how dark the subject matter, there's a laugh to be found underneath every stone. And if I'm the only one laughing then there's something wrong with everyone else, not me.

If you don't laugh about it, you'll cry about it.

The Grumpy Old Man

A big part of a doctor's development (and paperwork) is the idea that we self-reflect as we stumble through our own personal tumultuous and terrible tunnels of existence. How has my cancer and subsequent therapy affected, or even changed me? I guess the whole point of this memoir is to write this paragraph and I've spent most of my time complaining but hey, at least I'm writing it now!

So, what have I learnt? How have I become a better person? I've certainly changed my sense of humour in that I just don't care anymore. Well, I just don't care anymore less than before, anyway. I'm sure people have had hard times but it's not like they've had brain surgery, eh?

Maybe self-reflection is a load of crap and I should just re-read this memoir to determine who I've become instead of actually think about it?

I feel a lot older, in my mind and body. Idiots that rev their car engines at night piss me right off now, they didn't before. Well maybe they did, but not as much. My back hurts more, not sure if it's the physio and change to my posture (as in I have one now) or I'm just assuming the role of grumpy old man in my household.

I suppose actually I have a lot to reflect on, go figure. In some ways I'm very lucky to be alive and be able to do what I do now. A lot of people in my position are wasting away (or have already done so) so I know I should be grateful for what I have. My main drive/inspiration to stay alive and become human again, is of course the Wife and Boy. No exaggeration here but if I didn't have them, I would have just jumped off a bridge and saved the taxpayer the cost of issuing a blue disabled badge. Morbid but true.

In other ways I know that I've been dealt a shit hand. I've never smoked, taken drugs, abused alcohol (to a silly level anyway), worked in a factory full of asbestos or driven above the speed limit (ahem). At the beginning of this memoir, I said that I don't necessarily see myself as a good man. At the same time, I'm not sure I deserve what's happened to me. Am I selfish for saying that? Have I developed god-like powers overnight and the authority to decide who does and who doesn't get cancer?

I seem to ask more and more questions at the same time as I try to answer them. Maybe that's how you write a memoir?

THE END. FOR NOW

I guess every story has its end, and I've chosen this as mine. At this point I've managed to return to the real world, I'm at work but not part of the official rota yet. The process of getting back to work and how my symptoms are now could fill another volume, but I feel as if it's the next chapter in the book of my life. Therefore, I need to get to the end of that chapter before I look back on it.

Hopefully you've got to this point, and you haven't thrown this onto the fireplace, or, for our millennial readers, sent it to the Recycling Bin. This process started as a catharsis, a therapy for me to reflect and hopefully learn from the things that have happened to me. However, as I typed away it became clear to me that I wish I could have read this before I got ill. Nobody will sit down and discuss how constipated you'll become, but they're happy to discuss how your hair will fall out because that's what we see in films and on TV.

I would have paid a million pounds for someone to explain that I needed to take regular laxatives before I needed an enema... and there's your final image of me. For now.

PART 2

FOREWORD #2

I still don't think I'm a good man. I still laugh when fat people fall over, even if I suspect they've had brain surgery. I still don't think I'm necessarily a bad man either. The other day I helped an old lady cross the road. Okay that's a lie, I was driving, but at least I didn't run her over as she shuffled across the Zebra crossing (I'm awaiting my MBE).

On balance, I'm not even really sure I'm a good human being after all the self-reflection I've been doing. My latest horoscope told me I'm either capable of committing Genocide or raising a group of disabled orphans. Or maybe it said something like 'follow your intuition'. I didn't really read my horoscope, I'm not a flipping moron.

I guess what I'm trying to say is I've not yet worked out who I was before all this, how cancer changed me and in what direction I'm moving now. Maybe I've claimed to have done so in previous writings, but then why do I still have the urge to find myself on the back of an elephant in Thailand?

For the more astute out there you may have guessed that the reason you're sat here reading more of my vengeful hate, is because my cancer came back. And you'd be right, it had come back and I had more surgery as a result. Circumstances were different this time round, which is why I didn't just use copy and paste when analysing this macabre misstep in the dance of my life.

In the knowledge that I'm probably going to write more about my life from a retrospective perspective, I've decided to simply carry on from the point at which I stopped last time. That means the point at which I get diagnosed again will be a bit later on (is that probably the best bit? Should I have just started with that? Oh well...) I still have stuff to say that didn't make the last text either because I didn't need to go over it at that point or I simply couldn't be bothered. You decide which.

I confidently claimed earlier that I needed to live the next chapter of my life in order to look back. I just didn't think it'd be so soon... Since I last wrote I got more and more involved at work, my speech and walking both got slowly better and I gradually got around to the idea that I wouldn't be a helpless baby for the rest of my adult life. All admirable ambitions for an Alpha Male such as myself.

Post round two of cancer, I find myself thinking over some of the things that really bothered me from the first part of my memoir. I also find myself recalling what I did to try and alleviate some of those woes. So many things are better this time round, to lose acknowledgement of the past seems almost an insult to my previous efforts. 'Those who cannot remember the past are condemned to repeat it.' (George Santayana)

WAIT, YOU WANT TO GO BACK TO WORK?

Probably one of the biggest drivers in my recovery was the act of getting back to work. No, I'm not forgetting the impact of my family, of course they were my main reason for getting up in the morning. I'm saying that after getting out of bed, my ensuing incentive to survive was the act of returning to work. It became almost an obsession for me.

It all began when I was eight years old, selling lemonade from the pavement...

Scrap that, I'm not even fooling myself. Read on for what actually happened:

It began towards the beginning of my diagnosis when I said I wanted to go back to work as soon as possible. My Oncologist poured cold water over even the idea of me getting back to work, let alone soon. To be fair to him, I looked an absolute mess; I may even have been lying down in a hospital bed vomiting just as he entered the room – I wouldn't have trusted me with a coffee order, let alone a needle and syringe.

I suppose from a medic's perspective the prospect of me working as a Paediatric doctor, taking account of the fact that I needed help washing my own genitals in the shower, must have seemed far-fetched. I heard lots of very defeatist language from him about my condition; my nausea may be intractable (basically permanent), my speech may never be better than 'Sloth' from 'The Goonies' etc. Ok, maybe he didn't say exactly that.

I'm not writing this to say, 'nah nah nah, I don't get nauseous anymore and the only person that soaps up my bits is me!' I'm writing this because it inadvertently motivated me to get to work and stopped me from acting like a depressed teenager. My wife may protest that she was the one that stopped me weeping like a baby lamb and she may be right, but tough love is what I also needed, I guess.

WHAT AM I DOING?

The next few months I spent aiming at work like a missile. In hospital, I had more perspective on how far away that was but when I returned home in late January, I had a little devil on my shoulder telling me I was a no-good bum, sponging off family and the government alike, whilst my colleagues were at work, running around and pissing on huge fires. I began to believe that if I could get up from bed myself, eat a bowl of Coco Pops (other cereals are available to rot your children's teeth) and shower by myself; then I should be able to deal with an unwell child at work. Oh, and don't forget I was washing my own genitals at this point, in case that wasn't clear.

Well, I was wrong. Work was not around the corner for me. Vomiting on the sofa after having a shower was more of what was actually going on. I just wasn't ready physically. I was working closely with my Physiotherapist and Speech and Language Therapist at home, working on my movement and speech. I felt like I was training for the Olympics, except the training involved reading text out loud and trying to balance on one foot for five seconds. And at the end there was no competition, just my wife telling me how well I was doing. She has to say that, it says so in our marriage contract.

But what was I doing well for? Who was I doing all this for? I kept setting myself targets, 'I'll be back to work in a month' or 'I'll put up that shelf in the boy's room' or 'I'll clear R Kelly's name in court'. Maybe not all as realistic as I thought.

Targets and goals are important, and I feel writing them down helped me. Even if they were aspirational at best. When I wrote the words 'return to work' down I was miles away from it, like Sisyphus, the Greek king of Corinth pushing his boulder up a hill, only to have it roll back down when he reached the top.

THE DONKEY SYSTEM

So began a maelstrom of bureaucracy, emails and forms needed to get me back to work. Now I'm not going to badmouth the NHS system as a whole when it comes to returning to work. I'm not going to describe it as a donkey with one leg missing, constipated and working through a terminal cancer diagnosis. In slow motion.

No, I'm not going to do that.

But – If I was, I'd take that metaphorical donkey outside and shoot it in the head. Metaphorically of course.

Anything in the NHS that isn't considered 'stopping someone from being dead' is put on an imaginary conveyor belt of 'f**k it, I'll do it when I get to it'. It's a conveyer belt because each task is placed on the belt in order and yet each task is actually dealt with in order of ease or attractiveness of what you have to do. Also, it means someone else standing at the belt can offer to deal with the task and as a result; leave the first individual with absolutely no responsibility or obligation for their supposed objective.

Now if someone puts an unattractive task on the belt, such as getting a doctor back to work to help with an already dwindling workforce, well, that is dealt with in a specified time frame. As in it takes absolutely ages, you endure a glacial pace of effort, waiting for your emails to refresh or waiting for your phone to light up with a call. It takes much, much longer than you think would be sensible.

Now it's not always the fault of NHS admin staff, the system also relies on doctors reading their emails, replying in a timely manner and being generally organised. Now I don't mean organised to the point of satisfying someone with OCD, I just mean organised to the level of an eight-year-old opening emails on an iPad, perhaps.

This is something the majority of doctors fail to do day by day, often in a spectacular fashion. I'm being unfair here possibly, but it's generally male, Dinosaur Doctors who still think mobile phones were supplied by Nazis to take over our minds and that using the calculator on said mobile phones is somehow 'cheating'.

And don't think I'm generalising to be witty and spiteful; this is based on personal experience and observation over the years. To date, the NHS is the world's largest purchaser of fax machines. As in brand new fax machines. I think that tells you everything about how the NHS works behind closed doors.

I often lie through my teeth when colleagues ask me to fax something, I just repeat that the fax machine is broken until they give me their email address.

***

Here's an example of how difficult it became for me returning back to work: a part of any worker's return to a working environment after a period of illness, is that there needs to be some involvement from Occupational Health (OH). These individuals are employed by your employers and so have a vested interest in keeping you healthy and in work. By the same admission this grants them the power to restrict or even condemn your capacity to work even in the first instance. They can give or take away your responsibilities, and you can use them like a crutch, should you choose.

Almost like a child saying to their mother, 'it's ok, Daddy said I'm ok to use this deodorant can and fire lighter around the house'. By extension, you can say at work, 'it's ok, Occupational Health said I can use this deodorant can and fire lighter to treat my patients'. And no-one will bat an eyelid. Sort of.

Anyway, my employer followed convention plus my wishes and referred me to OH as far back as February 2019, only three months after my initial surgery. I've re-read emails from around this time saying how keen I was to return to work and how I was all fine etc etc. I was obviously not fine. I eventually got back to work in November of the same year – eight months after I was initially referred to OH.

So, I won't bore you senseless with the dates, but in-between February and November I had an OH doctor call me over the phone and ask me a few questions about my condition and how I get by day to day. It was a phone call because they set up a physical appointment flipping miles away from where I live, my wife was at work on that day and I wasn't allowed to drive. When I called to rearrange, they just asked the doctor to ring me instead.

He asked stuff like 'can you walk/run' 'how long can you hold your breath in a bucket of custard' and 'if you had to pick between Batman or Superman in a fight, who would you pick?'

I thought I answered diligently and honestly and I'm not actually sure what that doctor said about me and my capacity to return to work (can't find the damn report, must have been too close to 'he's a psychopath') but I was informed much later on in the year that I needed to see an OH doctor in the flesh, not just over the phone. And guess what, it took bloody ages to organise an appointment I could go to via taxi. Which meant my return to work was delayed by bloody ages as well.

All the while I was sat there at home, furiously reloading my emails, hoping somebody would contact me and say 'don't worry about the bureaucracy, let's just cut the bullshit, get you back in work and sort out all the boring bits later. After all, there aren't enough doctors working, we could use your help'. That would make sense wouldn't it?

Ok, so its mid-November and I've finally arranged a meeting between my work supervisor, a lead employer representative and some empty chairs. Oh, and of course my wife was there to stop me saying anything offensive or reveal any of my women's lingerie in the meeting. Of course, the meeting went fine, and it was agreed that I could start work the following week, on a phased-return basis. The plan was to start with one half day a week, increasing by another half day every week. This meant that by week six I would be doing six half days, or three full days. The target was ten half days or five full days: Monday to Friday. Simple. I just wish we'd got there weeks and weeks earlier...

I'm back at work at this point, supernumerary (basically means 'extra', I was shadowing other doctors) but wearing an ironed shirt and 'back'. There is a bit more between this point and my next operation, but I'll be honest and admit I'm a bit bored of talking about work. What I'll do is moan about some other things and then come back to it.

Stupid Man. Smart Home.

My next objective after being discharged from hospital all that time ago was making my home as comfortable as it could be for me and my family. Something I could do from my hospital bed was use my phone to trawl through the internet and research ways to automate and make my home (that I hadn't set foot in yet) as 'smart' as I was. Okay maybe a fair bit smarter.

Because I wasn't about to remodel the kitchen, trim the hedges or do anything actually useful, (it took a good few months to be trusted to take the bins out) I spent my time, money and energy buying 'smart' gadgets or threatening to do so.

This involved installing smart light bulbs in most rooms, Amazon Alexa-enabled devices littered across the house, Sonos speakers near anything with ears and a smart thermostat that you can programme with specific temperature ranges.

I put motion sensors in the entrance hallway so when you come into the house at night the light turns on automatically to guide your way. My thermostat turns itself off to save energy when it detects the mobiles that belong to me and my wife are away from the house.

In the same way a middle-aged man with thinning hair in a Widow's peak might buy a Porsche or a huge Range Rover; I filled my house with gadgets that saved me maybe four or five seconds of time a day. Did I use that time to better myself or the world around me?

Take a wild guess.

***

As well as all the useful practical applications, there's also the fact that you can create your own scripts or formulae, to make all the technology work together to help/annoy people.

This should turn you to my way of thinking: one night I lay next to my wife in bed as she was just drifting off. I stared at the ceiling and said 'Alexa, good night'. The speaker replied with 'Good night and get some beauty sleep, not that you need it!' Then the bedside lamp turned on to a dim, red light and Marvin Gaye's 'Let's Get it On' drifted out of the nearby speaker. Perfect...

Now, I expected a laugh or maybe an acknowledgment of just how much of a genius I am. A knighthood or even a small parade would have been fine.

Instead, I got white-hot rage; 'turn that f**king music off!'

Fair.

***

On a serious note, I did all this not because I'm addicted to wasting money (or 'investing in the future' as I meekly protest to my wife) but because in my infantile mind I thought having stuff turn on and off automatically would make our lives easier. It does to a point, when I proclaim 'Alexa! Turn on the bedroom lights' and they come on; I do feel like a god amongst men (blasphemous but it's the best feeling in the world when it works, trust me). The issue is my toddler is closer than I'm comfortable with to learning how to say 'Alexa, turn the heating up to forty degrees and release the hounds'.

The other serious and fairly sobering reason for surrounding myself with expensive gadgets was to make up for my lack of humanity. Now that is a truly histrionic statement, I'm aware, but not being able to walk or talk properly made me feel like I was in someone else's body – like an alien directing a bag of bones on how to shower properly.

As dramatic as I'm conscious I'm being, it doesn't change the fact that I felt like less of a man; and buying smart technology seemed to substitute my physical deficiencies. If it's difficult to get up from the sofa and turn the lamp on by hand, then I'll shout at Alexa to do it instead.

At the same time, I can't deny the fact that controlling lightbulbs from the sofa is badass, completely separate from the sensible(ish) things I listed above.

Wee Can Work It Out

Now for an actual physical, or maybe psychological problem that bothered me in a new, particularly annoying way. No, it's not the fact that I was so good looking that people wouldn't take me seriously (although every day it gets harder, sob sob). It was my bladder.

My problem started when I was in hospital after my first operation. All of a sudden, on one evening I just couldn't get to sleep due to the awkward sensation of needing a wee. So, I grabbed a Wee Bottle©®™ and relieved myself. Eyes closed, ten minutes later – shit. Need a wee. No more Wee Bottles©®™. Shit. Need a nurse. Hi nurse, I need a Wee Bottle©®™. Great. Relieved myself. Ten minutes later – shit. Need a wee.

You get the idea?

After maybe the third or fourth time I conceded my bladder was empty, and I was going mad. So, I did my best to ignore it and eventually got to sleep. This problem continued for maybe a few weeks and then simply melted away. I told my

Oncologist after it had improved, and we agreed to keep an eye on it and not initiate a State of Emergency just yet.

Now my dates and durations here are a bit fuzzy so you'll have to bear with me. At some point, the sensation came back when I was back in my bed at home, no idea why. I'd lie in my own comfy bed, kiss my wife good night and – shit. Need a wee.

***

There's a vicious rumour around that I might be some sort of scientist, and so therefore I tried to change things at home one after the other: less spicy foods, less to no caffeine during the day, not drinking past a certain point in the evening, less fluids during the day etc etc.

None of it worked and so I eventually admitted defeat and found myself in front of a Urologist in a hospital nearby. However, before I ended up there, I had to attend another clinic first, in order to demonstrate loyalty to the cult and prolong my suffering a little more first.

How to Look After Your Recorder

My first contact with the service was an appointment where they listened to my story, examined my bits and used a gadget to analyse the quality of my urine 'stream'. My reward for all this was another appointment where I was ordered into my boxer shorts and a hospital gown. I was taken through to a room, laid down on a hard death-slab plinth and - examined. More accurately, the inside of my bladder was examined to look for nasty things like cancers and the like. And the only way they could get inside the bladder was to insert a camera into the – err – right place.

I'll paint a picture for you. Do you remember being taught the recorder when you were little at school? Well, we were given the instrument of torture and instructed to go out and piss off as many parents as we could in the name of practising music. We did so but were also given a cleaning pipe as well; it's a long piece of pipe that you shove down the end of the recorder, move it about, side to side, in and out a bit until you can be sure your recorder is spick and span. Then, you never speak of what happened, to anyone. Ever again.

Well hopefully that cleared everything up. Where was I? All the tests were fine and so I went to go see the consultant Urologist who told me my symptoms were either because I was mad and imagining things (which I'm sure he was not keen to help me with) or more likely I had a condition called Overactive or Neurogenic Bladder. This means the brain is firing off the wrong electric signals to the bladder and trying to convince it that I needed a wee when I didn't. It's a disorderly, random and annoying condition and he could only guess at the cause. It could be the first operation, could be the radiotherapy, could even be just bad luck.

Thankfully the Urologist had some drugs up his sleeve which he gladly recommended. If they didn't work then the next option would be injecting Botox directly into the wall of my bladder, and apart from sounding like a barrel of laughs, it had a few nasty side-effects I'd rather avoid.

I tried the meds and either because I'm lucky or I stopped being mad, my symptoms have largely gone down the drain. See what I did there?

KING OF THE ROAD

Here's another reason to condemn me as a spoilt child, depraved of his toys: I wasn't allowed to drive from the end of my radiotherapy for a whole year. I love driving, my car is definitely one of my favourite toys (I have a dial that makes the engine noise sound more aggressive, judge me, I deserve it) and whilst I'm not a spoilt child – I paid for it with my own money/left kidney – I was definitely a deprived one.

Whilst I was properly gutted at not being able to drive off wherever I wanted, I could appreciate me driving at the beginning of the year would have been a pretty bad idea. Think Mad Max with Parkinson's, unable to turn his head from left to right without getting dizzy and throwing up.

A part of my petulant attitude towards not being able to drive was getting used to the fact that my wife effectively became the family chauffeur; I went from jumping into the driver's seat to shyly slinking into the passenger seat instead. I was very lucky to have her drive me and I'm fairly certain were the shoe on the other foot, I would have been tempted to buy her a bus pass and be done with it.

Now my wife is a competent driver and I do trust her to take our son to nursery or drop me off at the nearest Alternative Medicine Centre. I have to give a balanced view, however, of her mentality and general outlook on being behind the wheel: she's bat-shit-crazy. She would disagree with this and that's fine, some opinions aren't as correct as others.

She drives way too fast and when normal people see corners in the road my wife sees a challenge like she thinks she's Colin McRae. Which results in my nauseous stomach being lurched laterally somewhere into the road and my face turning green.

I did say I would be balanced so I'll say this: my mother is a – err, less than good – driver, my father is a confident but – umm, not very good - driver, my brother doesn't even drive and so really, I'm the only decent driver in this little Rat Pack. There you go, balanced view.

TAXI! TAXI!

Towards the end of my vehicular penance, I started to feel like I really could drive if needed. I was a couple of months away from being DVLA-approved to drive and so when I returned to work, I had to get taxis to and from work, about a six-mile journey each way. I got some help from the government to help pay for the taxis which was nice. The only issues were the taxis and drivers themselves...

Generally, the taxis were late in the morning. Once I had to wait forty-five minutes and then I sat in traffic for ages, so I got to work pretty late. Booking the taxis to come take me home after work was a similar ball-ache: I would order a taxi and then wait half an hour sat in the hospital main entrance. Patients and colleagues would walk past me thinking 'what's he sitting around waiting for? Should I give him some coins? He looks so fed up. Oh, he doesn't have a hat or guitar case to collect any money, let's just walk past quickly.'

***

The journeys themselves were either highlights in my day or massive downers. Here's a selection of rides I'll never forget, in order of increasing weirdness:

<u>Weird taxi Numero Uno</u> – strong smell of body odour coming from driver after a long day at work. So bad I made an excuse about opening the rear windows. After a while Sir Pongalot closed my window from the front – always an ominous sign when in a taxi – and a few minutes later must have felt he'd be arrested for Chemical Weapon usage and so opened both my window and his. I survived, yes, but I'm not sure my nostrils will recover.

Weird taxi Numero Dos – get into taxi early in the morning and sense instantly that my driver is a talker and so I instantly belt up and stare down at my phone. Now the details on exactly what was said next are sketchy, maybe due to shock, I think. And full disclosure: this taxi journey was both hilarious and horrifying (on reflection), but I also wish the man the very best, despite my description of events.

So, as I sat trying to avoid any dialogue, he asked me why I was in a taxi, not driving myself to work. I told him the gory truth about my cancer, and he said all the right things and I thought to myself, 'great, telling people I had a brain tumour usually ends most conversations'.

Except it did the opposite in this case and the poor man went on to tell me his life story: his wife died of cancer (pancreatic I think, horrible) and this sent him into a spiral of depression. He became estranged from his own children and especially his dead wife's family. He even told me his wife's coffin was coloured purple and cost him six thousand pounds. He told me about all the horrible things he was told by his wife's family after her death (I was counting every metre on the road by this point, but it was still very sad).

Just when I thought he couldn't have any more skeletons in the closet, he goes on to tell me about his daughter's breakdown and his son's misdemeanours from the law. If he told me he was Manchester's leading producer of marmite-flavoured edible underwear, I wouldn't have batted an eyelid.

I'm afraid there's no twist to the end of this tale, eventually we arrived at my work, I paid him and hurried off like a scared Church Mouse. Really, I should have made him pay me for counselling but that shows just how considerate I am.

Weird taxi Numero Tres – heading back home and this friendly-looking man picks me up and quizzes me on my job in the hospital. I resist the urge to tell him how much money I was making by supplying Graverobbers with body parts. I listen meekly to his ramblings about family members getting sick. I had nothing intelligent to add and couldn't have got a word in edgeways anyway.

Next, he began asking me if I knew this random old Asian man. When I replied in the negative, he told me at length about how this man had 'healed' loads of sick people when the hospital failed them. At this point I thought 'shit, he's not just hyper-active, he's mental' – but held my tongue (we were driving through a pretty rough area at this point and I preferred to stay inside the taxi). He told me meeting this old man had changed his life – but for the life of me I can't remember how exactly.

Now this doesn't sound totally bonkers on the page but trust me, sitting there listening to this man talk rapidly about an elderly witch doctor made me increasingly nervous. It reminded me of being sober and spending the night with someone who's getting progressively more drunk; they're not in control of what they're saying or who they bump into.

They're not censoring their opinions on how people with double-barrelled surnames are increasing in number and are slowly taking over middle-class Britain, and you're worried they're going to get in a fight soon and you've just walked into the wrong bar. Well, a very middle-class bar and a very middle-class fight albeit.

That's how I felt, 'he's working up to revealing he wants to cleanse the earth of heathens and he wants to start in South Manchester. My ticket's up at last'.

As I sat squirming, he managed to prod me into a discussion about politics. Normally I don't mind but soon regretted agreeing with everything he said because he then asked me who I thought was behind all of the world's political leaders? Who convinced Tony Blair to go to war or persuaded Donald Trump not to jump off the world's tallest building? The Illuminati? The Stone Masons?

Nope, 'it's Aliens bruv'. I said 'what?', 'yeh it's all Aliens bruv. Influencing all the major decisions in the world. The old man told me about it bruv'.

The next few minutes were a complete blur as all I could hear in my head was my own voice saying over and over 'shit he's crazy, shit he's crazy, shit he's crazy'. I caught angry ramblings about how he hated the taxi company and how they were all 'total bastards bruv' in-between more alien chat. He named people that had particularly offended him and how they were all 'total bastards bruv'. Luckily my house loomed into view and I made him drop me off a few hundred metres down the road, so he didn't watch me go into my house.

Should I have noted down his licence plate and called the taxi company/police and told them this man was having a psychotic breakdown?

Nah, I ran (well, staggered quickly) into my house, kissed my wife and son and checked all the locks.

What is it about my face? Why do people want to tell me these things?? I don't want to hear any things about anyone!

I'M BACK, BABY

Taxis to work ties in nicely with talking about work again, so maybe I'll do just that. There I stood in the hospital entrance on my first day in mid-November. I love working with children because it allows me to take a large step back from my everyday adult way of thinking, the cursing and maelstrom of all-encompassing and all-consuming negative emotions. It allows me to shift my perspective to a more positive and well, child-like view on life and health. Being around children not only stops me from writing terrible things in a memoir (there's more to come don't worry), it grounds me and makes me happy inside and out. I am a very lucky boy.

It felt good wearing an ironed shirt and new leather shoes. The red carpet, confetti and Brass Band awaiting my arrival was a nice touch. Oh wait – maybe it happened a little differently. Fuzzy memory and all that.

As detailed before, over the next couple of months I came into work more and more each week, performing the duties expected of a doctor at my level. I went on ward rounds, helped my colleagues with jobs on the wards (mainly paperwork, phoning/annoying people and taking blood samples), attended outpatient clinics and sat in the office doing more paperwork or phoning/annoying people again.

I was particularly proud of the fact that I slowly got back to taking bloods. Luckily, I'm right-handed (and I had issues with my left hand, more later) but the first couple of times I stabbed a needle into a child's arm I shook like a house made of sticks in an earthquake. I persuaded the children to look at the opposite wall to distract them, but I could feel the eyes of the parents burrowing into my soul. Thankfully I got blood on the first attempt for the first few episodes, resulting in a few less shakes when re-attempted, mainly riding on the wave of confidence.

HANDLE WITH CARE

My arrival back to work was heralded before I arrived. Most of the department knew I was coming and I'm not sure to what extent, but they knew I wasn't at 100%. Everyone in the know was extremely nice to me and I never felt that I was being put into a difficult position. Little things like 'oh let's get the lift instead of the stairs' or 'I'll take this form downstairs myself later, don't worry', prompted my suspicions that someone had branded me as 'delicate goods, handle with care'.

No-one around me asked too many questions. Well maybe a couple of people, and I appreciated that, but on the whole people seemed content with not rocking the boat. Not that I would have minded talking about what's happened to me, otherwise I wouldn't be writing this!

I suppose more than just rabbiting on about myself, I wanted to explain to people why I looked like a broken rag doll when moving around the hospital. One colleague asked me directly what had happened to me and then said, 'yeah, we did think it was something Neurology-related from the way you walked'. Which was fine but I assume that meant that my supervisor hadn't given anyone any details other than 'he was sick'.

On those lines I wanted to assure people that my symptoms were from a tumour; not something like a massive overdose of heroin or something I'd rather keep to myself. I'm not sure what the management would say if I walked around with a label on my chest that said 'I had a brain tumour which explains why I look like I'm pissed. For all abuse/enquiries please phone my wife on 075********'.

ELEPHANT IN THE ROOM

My other colleagues in other departments were a mixed bag. Some knew a tiny bit more about me than others, most remembered me from the last time I worked in that hospital and some just thought I was taking the piss out of children with Cerebral Palsy.

Some people were lovely and told me how well I was doing, others I could tell just wanted to leave me to it. And that was fine. I didn't want it to define me, so I just carried on, speaking funny yes but mainly just getting on with the job, giving people less reason to see me as anything other than a worker bee. And I've been saying that all along, I just wanted to get back to where I was, no matter what I had to do or how long it would take.

I recall attending an educational course with a load of other medics, nurses and physios. At lunch I got chatting to an old doctor colleague I worked with a couple of years previously. We had as normal a conversation as two doctors can have (the phrase 'we don't get paid enough for this shit' must have been dropped at some point, just by the laws of probability) and at some point, I made a reference to my time off sick. He acknowledged it and there was something about the way he just took it in his stride made me ask him, 'do you know why I was off?'

He patted me on the shoulder and said something like 'yes don't worry I know'. I was confused because I hadn't seen him or any associated colleagues for ages. He told me the paediatric trainees in the area were a small group and 'word gets around'. I wonder what's been said? Maybe I should have taken the opportunity to spread something like, 'I heard he had surgery on his left big toe and reattached it his forehead' or 'I heard he was hung like a horse'.

EH?

One of my biggest fears when returning to work was people not being able to understand me. That or run out of patience when I spoke too slowly and start looking around the room like they're trying to find a poster on the wall that will explain everything I was saying, only quicker and with pictures. Or maybe that's just what I do when someone at work speaks to me...

At first, I would try to get away with smiling and nodding, something every married man learns the second the wedding's over. But eventually I found myself alone with patients and their parents; their attention fixed on the bullshit coming out of my mouth. It's an interesting and unique relationship between a doctor and patient; as the doctor you want to help/advise so you assume you have a captive audience. As a patient or parent, you want to help yourself (or your child although you shouldn't just assume this is the case!) and therefore nine times out of ten whatever comes out the doctor's mouth you take seriously.

This helped immeasurably in my case. Yes, I received the odd 'eh?' at the end of a sentence but I didn't mind repeating myself. Mainly because during my time as a patient I would find myself going 'eh?' in my head, even though I have a head start as a medic.

Generally, people listened to my every word, even if I stumbled over some (I've listened to a recording of myself saying 'medication' and I just went 'eh?'). I could see it in their faces when their brow furrowed, they were thinking 'why have they sent me a medical student with a learning disability?' However, after listening to me speak for a minute or so they soon relaxed in their chair. I was telling them how I was going to make their child feel better, so they were on my side in the end.

During my time at work, I never had to give out any bad news like telling a five-year-old they had cancer, so I guess that's the next real challenge for me and my big mouth. I can just picture it now; 'ok Timmy, I'm afraid you have foot cancer. We're going to have to amputate'.

'Eh?'

So Close.

Being in work was a unification for me. It brought together a lot of my grievances into one place and allowed me to lurch from one point to another at a reasonable pace. I love working with children, I would have followed any work schedule if it helped me get closer to where I was.

My supervisor was supportive, he let me get on with it and tolerated my timetable of increasing hours every week. Well, I guess I was extra in the numbers, so he didn't have to worry when I wasn't there, but still.

The plan from OH was to increase my weekly hours to five full days a week with no on-calls. The next part of the plan was to start to work on the normal rota from the beginning of March. This meant I was no longer supernumerary or an extra in the numbers, the only thing I was following was my own shadow.

The other aspect of the plan was to begin to work on-call shifts in the evenings, shadowing another doctor. This went fine, although I only managed two on-call shifts before all the cards fell down around me. I worked a couple of weeks at this new level, I even spent one day showing the ropes to my new colleague working the same job as me.

Then I got my news and was never seen again... Well, maybe not in that specific role but I survived at least to this point of writing this memoir.

So many Coronavirus Jokes out there, it's a Pundemic.

Now I want to talk about my new diagnosis, the operation that followed and how it turned my world upside-down again — however, I need to speak a little bit about what was happening around that time and how it affected almost every aspect of my upcoming ordeal. Namely, COVID-19, or the deadly Coronavirus.

Depending on when you're reading this, COVID-19 could either be a distant memory or a hellish reality. I'll break it down as simply as I can.

In early 2020 the world started to get seriously nervous about a new flu-like-illness originating from the East. Most people stuck their head in the sand and pretended nothing was happening, me included. Then the death toll across the globe started to rise and the stakes changed.

Some people went out and bought huge bags of pasta or rice in preparation. These people were either sensible people reading the news every day and then spending a little extra on their normal weekly shop. Or they were bat-shit-crazy individuals that have garden bomb shelters in their search history. Whatever the motivation, it turned out to be the right call.

My wife bought loads of extra stuff for us; I'm still trying to work out her thought process, but she did well in the end. I mean she is bat-shit-crazy on a good day (you know this already right?) but maybe she was inspired by a moment of lucidity?

It all kicked off properly in mid-March-ish. People had been panic buying in supermarkets and keeping their distance from people as if the Plague had come back. My wife said she saw an Asian woman in Lidl packing her trolley with ten baguettes. I mean, how thick was that woman? Those baguettes will be inedible in a matter of days (unless she had like ten children, in which case she really was thick). When I become Emperor of the World, she'll be one of the first to be sacrificed. Her and whoever stole my bike when I was twelve years old.

A note about the virus: COVID-19 was a highly infectious organism, however it's not as dangerous as other infections, such as Ebola for example. Essentially, it's good at spreading from person to person but it doesn't always kill you. A fit and healthy adult may have very mild symptoms and get over it at home with some Paracetamol and a bowl of Mum's Chicken Soup. Or, you're fit and healthy, yet you contract the virus and then die weeks later in a hospital bed when your lungs fail to work, and your body shuts down. So, it was infectious and unpredictable.

More concerning was the fact that many infected individuals were symptom-free and were walking about without a care, infecting others unknowingly. You might think this Diet-Coke virus doesn't sound that dangerous, but the elderly and unwell in our society were slowly dying off. Advice came from the government; 'if you have any flu-like symptoms then stay at home for a couple of weeks', essentially reducing the risk that these people wander into a nursing home and cough over everyone and everything.

***

Just like Lord of the Flies or The Hunger Games, when faced with adversity, the fundamental principles that determine human behaviour come into play: kill or be killed. Or join a group that will do the killing for you and observe.

I'm putting my reductionist hat on here, but I truly believe our population divided itself into two camps: dickheads and non-dickheads. Most people kept their distance from people, observed the rules on isolating if needed and held back from buying ten f**king baguettes in Lidl.

Others were not so altruistic. YouTube began to fill with videos of empty shelves in the toilet paper section of supermarkets. Young people gathering in large groups, flouting the rules and essentially increasing the infectivity rate across the country. Some countries employed a much more resolute policing policy – throw a party for a hundred people in your tiny inner-city flat and we'll crack your flipping skull open.

England has been gradually reducing police numbers over the past few years under Conservative rule and allowing the general public to do/say what they want. I'm all for civil liberty and rights blah blah blah but the result in this country was a populace running wild in the towns and cities, sneezing at the elderly and selling toilet paper on eBay for twenty quid a roll.

Now I find it much more enjoyable and satisfying to paint a literary picture of the Apocalypse, our world falling apart around us like a Digestive biscuit left in a cup of tea for too long. However, in reality, things became slowly better, the country went into a more stringent lockdown state and the death toll began to decrease. It became a social norm to challenge people that weren't following the rules; now videos were emerging of people shouting at teenagers that were meeting en-masse in parks. Supermarkets began to stock more toilet paper and it seemed things were more under control.

WHY SHOULD I CARE?

Now I'm assuming you're wondering why I'm auditioning for the BBC News, essentially keep in mind what was happening in the world as I continue below. COVID-19 was integral in the decisions regarding my care from the moment I was diagnosed.

More relevant to my situation was the order from the government that people with 'chronic medical conditions or cancer' should isolate for three months or so. Basically, the weak, frail and any other high-risk individual with a chronic medical condition. My issue was straightforward, 'do I still have cancer and am I considered high-risk?'

I didn't have very long to ponder the question; within a few days I had my next outpatient appointment with my Oncologist. It was a Wednesday morning, I planned to go into hospital, have my blood test, come home and speak to my consultant over the phone (a family member of his had flu-like symptoms and so he was working from home with access to my medical records). I expected to be told everything was fine and I'd even planned to go into work later that morning.

'Your latest brain scan is showing something. We need to find out what it is.'

Oh.

THE FALLOUT

I've never been dumped before over the phone but I'm assuming it's similar to what happened to me then. My consultant was pleased to learn I had no new symptoms, and my blood tests were fine. He then said something about discussing my case at a meeting with other experts and telling me the 'something' could be nothing, scar tissue from my previous operation for example... But I knew what it was. I knew what was sneaking back into my life like a thief in the night. My wife put on a brave face, but she knew what I knew.

Goes without saying but I didn't go back to work after that. I knew my next port of call was more brain surgery. I remember asking my consultant if I'm 'high-risk' or not considering my last treatment was a while ago. He decided I was so in that instant I was a 'high-risk individual', and I was self-isolating at home. That is, as long as I survived the next bit.

***

I'm trying to recall exactly what was running through my head when I was first told I had a brain tumour. I then tried to draw parallels to the experience I had second time round. I think I used the word 'numb' to describe the first time. I think it describes how I felt this time as well.

My wife's hand went to my knee, it was her news as well as mine, after all. Telling someone they have cancer is probably the most poignant piece of news-giving we learn about giving at medical school. That and 'you have a Sexually Transmitted Infection sir. I understand you couldn't possibly have contracted it yourself, yet your genital warts did not come from thin air, so I suggest you aim some of your emotions away from me and have a think about your movements in the last few days.'

How Do You Operate on a Dodo?

So, there I was, holding my wife's hand on my knee, saying 'yes', 'ok', 'thank you' to my phone when really my mind was stepping backwards over a cliff-edge and I could do nothing about it. My thoughts were: 'I'm going to die, I'm going to die, I'm going to die'. In my limited experience when cancer reoccurs it's usually a bad thing and you hardly ever hear, 'ooo yes his cancer came back, but he survived it just like the other seven times.' I hear more often 'ooo yes he's dead as a Dodo now, the cancer came back and it was just too much for him.'

I got it into my mind that this was a disaster and every month or so I would grow a new tumour and each operation or treatment would leave me more and more disabled until a group of vultures decided to perch permanently on a branch near my window, waiting for me to pop my clogs.

In reality what they suspected was a new cancer, was a small growth on the edge of where my original tumour used to be. In that case it was a smaller operation and therefore a smaller problem.

The next week I got phone calls from both my Oncologist and Neurosurgeon (the same man who had operated on me over a year ago). Essentially the meeting of experts had concluded that 'yes, that's a tumour. Take it out please.' My surgeon asked me to come and see him in clinic the next day.

MEETING OF MINDS

The experience was surreal, everyone was instructed to wash their hands thoroughly upon entering the hospital and told to keep at least two metres away from everyone else. All in the name of preventing transmission of the virus. I went with both my father and wife, just in case any local street gangs decided to kick off during my visit. All the chairs in the outpatient waiting room were moved two metres apart so it looked like a weird slalom race to the consulting rooms.

I was only allowed to take my wife into the clinic room with me, my father confined to the waiting room like a naughty schoolchild. Inside the room my wife and I sat a metre or so away from the desk and my surgeon sat behind it, replete with mask, gloves and an 'I'm sorry but I'm not allowed to shake your hand' kind of look on his face.

Essentially the appointment was to explain to me that I'm going to have more brain surgery on a smaller area than last time. He confirmed it would be a smaller operation and therefore, hopefully a shorter recovery time.

The biggest issue was what to do about the COVID-19 outbreak. His dilemma was that he wanted to operate sooner rather than later but there was a much higher risk to me than last time. As well as potentially contracting the virus in my weakened state; there was the fact that staff members were going off sick and self-isolating left, right and centre. The government advice at the time was if anyone in your household develops any new symptoms then the whole household has to stay home and self-isolate for at least a couple of weeks. That included nurses and other staff scheduled to work on the neurosurgery ward.

I had another MRI scan booked two days after my appointment. The deal was if it looked worse, I'd have surgery pronto. If same or better, then we could wait. I think he said after the virus had passed, we could revisit it. That could've been months!

Two days later I had my operation. I seem to remember my scan wasn't massively different, but my surgeon had just found out he was operating on the Sunday when he previously thought he had a day off. So, he slotted me into the list and there I was, bright and early at seven am, having fasted since the previous night, ready for adventure.

My mother was looking after my son and so my wife and father came with me to hospital. I was quiet, unlike last time; I knew exactly what was coming. Just like when I was seventeen and had my driving test, I was not going to be a happy bunny.

LONELY COMPETITION WINNERS

We sat outside the surgical department, a few metres away from another man and his relative. I could tell instantly from the vacant look on his face that he was the brain surgery competition winner, not the lady sat with him. I wonder how my face looked?

Before long a nurse appeared on the corridor and announced she was taking me and the other man away. The hell? I was going alone? Turns out the hospital had updated their policies so that visitors weren't allowed anywhere near the operating theatre or waiting room. I knew things were getting bad with COVID-19 but I hadn't factored this in. I suddenly felt extremely vulnerable.

Last time I was operated on, my wife came into the anaesthetic room to be with me as I fell asleep. No such treatment this time.

So, I said my pathetic goodbyes (what are you supposed to say in a situation like this? See you in your nightmares, mwahahaha!) and promised to see my family as soon as the operation was over.

'Oh no, no visitors on the ward at all.' The hell?!? Last time I was in hospital for almost three months! I can't do this without my family!!!

***

But off I went regardless with the nurse after a terrified look back at my family. I wouldn't see them now until my discharge, whenever that would be. So off we went; me, the nurse and the other poor man going along in single file like Snow White's dwarves, 'Hi ho, hi ho, it's off to brain surgery we go!'

We were seated in a bed space (with a big gap between us obviously) and asked to change into a surgical hospital gown. True to form, I ignored the other man straightaway and pulled my curtain across. I told myself I had to finish my magazine before my operation because I might be dead or, like last time, not be physically able to read for weeks.

I finished my magazine and went for a nervous wee, giving a sad smile to the man as I passed. A small part of me wanted to comfort him, but then another part of me thought I'd probably just cause him anxiety about how he'll turn out after surgery. I overheard his chat with the surgeon when he came around (FYI in the NHS it's assumed that when you pull the curtains there's some sort of sci-fi sound barrier that envelops you and no-one else can hear your conversation. This is not true).

He was having his first operation on a different type of tumour in a different part of the brain to me. I've no idea if he's still with us but if he's anything like me he won't have heard even half of what was said to him by the surgeon. Still, he was in good hands and I hope he'd had plenty of time afterwards to ask what was going on.

THE GREAT ESCAPE

I suppose I should talk about the operation itself but – surprise surprise – I was asleep, so I'll skip forwards to the part where I woke up. And it was weird. I woke up and didn't vomit everywhere. I woke up and felt like moving around a bit and not wanting to punch someone in the face.

What was going on?

Oh. I must be dead.

But where was Beyoncè? Why weren't my feet being rubbed?

Then, I'm a bit sketchy on the details, but I think a nurse must have taken my blood pressure or something and brought me crashing back to earth. I was alive. I reached to the back of my head and felt the stiches on my elongated scar. I moved my legs, but they felt like lead, so I gave up. I moved my head to the left, and then to the right – no vomit.

I was out of the hospital on day three. I had some conditions I had to fulfil before I left though: Not look like I was going to die imminently and be able to walk 'independently'. I looked much better than the last time I had surgery. Eating and drinking wasn't a problem, my speech and vision seemed unchanged and I was slightly nauseous but not dizzy and vomiting everywhere like last time.

I gave the performance of my life when the Physiotherapists came around to see me. I swung my legs off the bed, put my trainers on (with a bit of help, God I miss Velcro as a child) and walked out of my room with my entourage. I summoned all my fortitude to traverse the length of the ward corridor and then we headed to the stairs. Somehow, I managed to go up and down a flight of stairs, and even back to my bed. I passed their test, but I suspect they moved the goalposts at least a couple of times to get me over the finish line.

This tied into the hospital/medical profession's ethos of 'if you ain't got COVID-19, then get the hell out of Dodge'. So, the physio report and the friendly registrar's collusion got me discharged on day three. I had a bag full of meds of course and instructions on how the stiches in the back of my head would be removed. But no Goody Bag with birthday cake inside.

WHAT HAVE I BEEN LET OUT TO?

So, no cake, and my father greeted me at the door to the ward, already having a full-blown argument with a nurse, trying desperately to tame the beast. I assume he was upset at not being able to get on the ward to pick me up, but I just wanted to get out of there, so I ushered him out of the door like a Metallica fan at a Justin Bieber concert, 'trust me, you don't want to be here'.

Just a note detailing the world I stepped out into after my incarceration. Around the time I went into hospital the UK was ordered into lockdown after weeks of messing about from the government. There remained the advice to keep a couple of metres away from people and lock yourself in a panic room should you develop a fever or cough.

A more recent conspiracy theory describes that the government delayed these lockdown rules on purpose to try and kill off a few more of the elderly and infirm, in order to build up some natural herd immunity in the population before ordering a stay-at-home order. If true I must have slipped through the net...

The lockdown meant people were advised to stay at home with whoever lived there, only leaving for essential travel (as in grocery shopping) or one trip for exercise (a run or bike ride, not dogging like I initially thought). Therefore, when I arrived home, I simply moved from one cage to another. Of course, the food was much better in the house-cage.

SHOULD I STAY OR SHOULD I GO?

I was so happy to be driven home and that I wasn't in hospital for anywhere near as long as last time – but in a way that turned out to be disadvantageous in some ways. My walking and general co-ordination were shocking. I told you I walked on my own with the physios in the hospital, but I assure you, I've never concentrated more on pretending to be able to walk in my life. On leaving the hospital I could barely complete a few steps without someone holding my arm. I resembled one of those army amputees with two new prosthetic legs, learning to walk. At the risk of making this sound like the sequel to an action film; I went from the highest peak to getting knocked back down again. I went from Terminator to broken tin soldier. I just had no heart, man.

So why was coming home early a potentially bad thing? Essentially over a year ago I stayed in hospital for ages and re-learnt to walk from my hospital bed. That meant I barely left the horizontal position except for when the physios came around. This time, I re-learnt to walk at home, with the concerned nurses and physios replaced with my family. Well, my toddler was f**king useless of course, but I'll let him off. For now.

STUNT MAN TRAINING CAMP

I fell over a fair bit. Not in a comic way like a baby learning how to walk (well, depends if you know who the baby is to be fair). More like 'ooh, that's gotta hurt'. The issue was of balance and co-ordination. I looked like a beached whale when trying to get up from the floor or sofa. My muscle tone can't have been too dissimilar from what it was the day before my operation and so therefore it was my nervous system that was giving me grief.

Once I was stood up with a lot of 'I'm ok, I'm ok, leave me alone', I would take a couple of steps and then 'oof' – I was back on my arse with a sore hip or, if I was lucky, slumped back on the sofa with only an embarrassed look on my face. I haven't injured myself particularly badly, except a bruised backside and ego.

It's a difficult thing, explaining just how dehumanising it is falling over all the time. On one hand you have everyone around you on tenterhooks, watching your every shaking, shuffling step. It made me feel like a monkey at the zoo, minus the screaming/throwing of faeces.

On the other hand, I suddenly felt like I was stuck in the mud, I couldn't go anywhere I wanted for fear of really hurting myself. Without being too melodramatic, I had lost my freedom to prowl the Savannah, lost my autonomy. After over a year since my last operation I'd been building myself up physically, from Zero to Hero, from wheelchair-bound to thirty seconds on a normal bike in a park with my wife nervously looking on.

Well, maybe the physical specimen you have in your head isn't quite how the mirror saw me, but it doesn't change the fact that I was able to drive to hospital, walk in and sign all the papers I needed before surgery. After surgery I staggered out the hospital, significantly less mobile than the man who walked in.

As I type, things are slowly getting better in that I've moved from Human Puddle to Human Jelly. Slightly more stable.

I used to measure my achievements in units such as winning against friends in a tennis match or attempting a recipe from a confusing cookbook (middle-class iz I innit). Now I think to myself, 'didn't fall over today. I walked to the fridge, back to the sofa and planted my backside all by myself. I am physical perfection personified'. Little victories.

***

When I managed to find my way to a sofa or chair without having a meeting with the floor, I thought I was fine. Then my other friends came to play. Nausea/vomiting, fatigue, bowel disturbance and my shaky, breaky hands.

My Invisible Nemesis

My first visitor was nausea. During my time in the hospital bed, I felt nauseous but nothing like before. I moved around a lot less than the week before the operation, certainly, but even so I didn't vomit once. I went home. Slept one night and then violently threw up the next morning.

It seemed my body was playing one last cruel joke though, because then my nausea all but abated and I had no more vomiting episodes. One of the most crippling and frankly depressing features of my last recovery period, my invisible nemesis, had transformed into a kitten with a ball of yarn. I use that example because I hate cats.

***

I went a good while without feeling nauseous again, until my second round of chemo, when my body played another couple of cruel jokes on me (not one to follow the rules). I vomited at least a couple times in the middle of the night and then in the morning. Still, nothing like before.

You're Tired? Well, I'm Tired of Hearing It

Fatigue was there again, silently waiting in the corner of the room; waiting for me to get up off the sofa and attach lead weights to my legs as I walked up and down my garden. I guess it was to be expected, my operation still took a good three hours despite being a much smaller job than last time and so there'll inevitably be a 'fatigue' period.

Why mention it if it'll get better on its own? Well it's worth saying that when you're learning to walk (for the third time in my life, not something I'm keen to relive again), you're concentrating on one foot in front of the other or heel-drop then toe-lift. It almost makes you want to cry when your body says, 'all this stuff is interesting but I'm tired now so march your sorry arse to that bench, or shuffle there, I don't mind.' Then you're sat there, huffing and puffing like an asthmatic at the top of a hill. 'Round two tomorrow I think'.

Everything is affected by fatigue, from the obvious 'I'll come out on a walk next time' you tell people, to the more subtle example of binge-watching something boring on TV, because you don't have the physical strength to get up and either grab the remote from the shelf or go outside. You don't have the mental stamina to go and do something better with your time. So, you sit there, sinking into the sofa as if it's quicksand, waiting for the end of the day to come around.

A good example of how the mundane became a daily struggle was with my walking up and down the stairs in my home. Bearing in mind I was in lockdown, so every day the stairs took the form of my literal and metaphorical mountain, for lack of real, outdoor challenges.

Let me paint a picture, from me standing at the top of the stairs. There I am, brave explorer peering down through a thick layer of clouds, ready to descend the precarious peak. Left foot lands on the first step, 'doing alright here', right foot goes up into the air and − shit − left leg locks straight and right leg wobbles as it expected the left leg to stay bent, not straighten up all of a sudden. So out goes left hand to grab the bannister and prevent disaster. 'I'm ok, I'm ok', reset limbs, take a deep breath and continue on.

So, now the right foot lands on the first step, 'doing alright this time', left foot goes up into the air and – shit – now the right leg locks straight and left leg wobbles. So out goes right hand to steady myself on the wall. 'I'm ok, I'm ok', reset limbs, take a deep breath and continue on, all the way to the bottom of the mountain.

Stiff drink at the bottom, drunk by lunchtime.

WOBBLE WOBBLE

Have you ever dropped something, like a mug of coffee that you were damn sure was in your hand? You reach behind you, feel that familiar handle, move it across your body and then – splash! – it's on the floor or your crotch? Or, you're using one hand to take a tray out the oven, you forget the hand you're using is a shaking mess and then – crash! – it's on the floor and you come out with, 'I don't got it...' Disappointing groans all round.

For me the offender was my left hand. Luckily, I'm right-handed otherwise my writing or competitive sewing would have been a right-off. I'm about as ambidextrous as an amputee.

I can't remember if it was mainly in one hand the last time but here I am now, the Terminator with only one good arm, no gadgets, weapons, inhuman strength or speed. So pretty much I was nothing like the Terminator – pretend you didn't read that - basically my left arm was next to useless whilst my right was alright-ish.

Despite my right arm being alright-ish, have you ever tried to tie your shoelaces with one 'alright-ish' hand while the other looks on apologetically? On top of that your legs are made of lead and you have to use the opposite hand to drag your foot up on your opposing knee in order to put your shoes on? You should try it. Endless fun.

***

Another personal tragedy of mine: my son likes to throw things around the house. Shock horror, he also likes to throw food on the floor, point at it and go 'ma dinna??'

One auspicious lunchtime we'd finished our meal and I'd spotted one lonely baked bean on the kitchen floor, ready to be squashed into oblivion on the bottom of someone's sock. I was carrying some plates or something in my right hand and so bent down and attempted to pick up the bean with my left thumb and forefinger. The little bastard decided to develop some sort of oily, slippery outer shell that sprang away from my shaky fingers the second I went near it. I think it must have escaped my grasp about eight times before I stood up and took stock.

Now, the sensible thing for someone of my intellectual standing would have been to put the plates down and reattempt the baked bean extraction with my right hand. But that would have been admitting defeat, so I carried on regardless, my chest hair and Man Points growing in number with each failed attempt. Eventually, of course, like the inevitable flow of time, I gave up and used my right hand to clear away my shame.

I essentially altered the way I used my hands to hide my deficiencies. Subtle things to make me less conspicuous: I only really carried things in my right hand and therefore clearing dinner plates would take two or three journeys as my left hand would either follow me round like a bad smell or I'd carry something light with it like a plastic cup. If I was tipping spices into a spoon in my right hand I would either guestimate the amount with my right hand or just give up and pretend we didn't have that ingredient. The second method was simpler but gingerbread cookies without ginger gave the game away a bit.

Invisible Inadequacies

For all the moaning I like to do there are people out there who have one or more limbs blown off in some faraway land and to listen to me whine about my arm must be infuriating. I get that. Some people have had strokes and their arm/leg isn't just different, it's completely dead. I get that.

I may have touched on this subject before, but you can spot an ex-soldier in a wheelchair with one arm a mile off. Stroke victims are a bit easier to spot because they might have weakness down the whole left or right side, including their face. Or more likely you'll notice that they're flipping old (with great age comes greater risk of strokes).

My 'temporary deficiencies' (my wife has tempered my use of the phrase, 'things that make me look like a cripple on Spice') are unfortunately not as visible as the above examples. Just as an aside and if you're too middle-class to know what Spice is, please Google 'Spice zombie Thriller' and watch the video. I hope you can appreciate it's not me in the video with the blurred face, but watching it took me a while to be sure, based on the way I move...

I'm sure if you put an ex-soldier in a wheelchair with only one arm in my position and asked them to write a memoir, they would probably wish for less visibility, 'I wish I had a brain tumour that resulted in shaky hands and a walk that makes me look like that farmer guy that gets possessed by an alien in the first Men in Black film'. Or something to that effect. I'm fairly sure they might be tired of people taking one look at them and forming an instant opinion.

The difference with my situation is people look at me, especially if I'm sat down, and think, 'he doesn't look like a cripple on Spice'. Thank you very much m'lady. But then I might stand up or drop some papers from my left hand and I can see 'maybe he does look like a cripple on Spice' sitting glumly behind their eyes. Then the moment of mutual trust is gone, and I think to myself that maybe next time I should wear a sign on my head advising people I may fall to the floor if the wind picks up. Or I talk funny because I've been possessed by an alien. Anything to break the ice really.

Wooaaahh

In the last part of my memoir, I talked about not being able to lie down and look to the ceiling or even the left side of the room. This time I was spared the indignity, partially. Before my second operation I'd managed to train my brain to behave itself when I lay down and stared at the ceiling. Post-second surgery I would lie down in bed, look up and endure a few seconds of my head spinning and a flood of nausea would descend from the top of my head down to the pit of my stomach.

It triggered my memories of being in a wave pool when I was younger. You think you're going to be ok and then 'wooaaahh', an artificial wave crashes over you and leaves you disorientated and flapping around in the water.

Thankfully, this wave in bed would be mitigated within a few seconds with some deep breathing and some mental coaching (please don't throw up, please don't throw up).

CONSTIPATED PERSONALITY = CONSTIPATED STORYLINE

My last visitor to this depressing party is 'bowel disturbance', or to put it plainly, 'I got constipated again and revisited a world of agony and cursing'. This was all at home this time as opposed to avoiding the toilet in the hospital room.

A few days into being at home I got the familiar abdominal pains and messages from my brain (or maybe the other end?) asserting, 'drop everything, go find a toilet'. And that I did, spending the next three hours in Tartarus, begging my wife through the door for laxatives or a Priest to come and read me my last rites. Whichever appeared first.

My wife soon asked if I wanted an enema, I said 'no I'll be ok', as if Man Points could be exchanged for a normal bowel movement. I heard her have a look at our left-over medication stash in the attic (right next to the dead bodies) – no enemas. Then I heard her go out to the pharmacy and return a while later. She asked me again if I needed the enemas and I finally conceded. Did I use them, or did I emerge from the bathroom without any further help, triumphant in my conquest over human physiology?

No. I did not. I used two.

DEADULTISED

Now that I've gone through the signs/symptoms that have characterised my time post-surgery, I find myself musing about the impact of my 'temporary deficiencies' on my life. I've done a lot of musing over this laptop, a few tears, a few bad memories and maybe even some good ones.

Life is shit, there's no doubt about it. I believe we're born to achieve one of two things: 1) Build and support your own family; wife, two kids and a house with a picket fence blah blah blah. Have a stable job, don't sacrifice baby goats to The Dark Prince etc etc.

2) Do something world-changing; create the cure for the common cold, become a famous triangle-player in an international orchestra, design the first bicycle with laser cannons attached or make everyone happy and assassinate Donald Trump (especially Melania).

I honestly don't think one approach Trumps the other (I just can't be stopped). To create life, a family, a legacy, is an amazing thing in itself and can be difficult at times.

Some people do both. Fine. It's likely those people will either become serial killers or dentists but the majority of us peasants will pick either option 1) or 2). In my late university years when I worked out that life was indeed shit, I made the decision that option 1) would make me happiest — and it has so far.

Except obviously for the cancer. It hasn't especially altered my main life ambition; it's just made getting there much harder. I find not having control of all aspects of my physical world utterly unbearable. Dehumanising. Demasculinising. Deadultising (I know this isn't a word, but it should be).

I can hear the world's smallest violin being played and I appreciate the word 'dehumanising' is more appropriate for the state of the poor people who were kept in Auschwitz, for example. But I defend its usage when describing my own existence, because it's my personal feeling and it's the way I see myself when my own mother has to help me stand up from a park bench.

ULTIMATELY ALTERED

Doubtless some aspects of my physical condition would make an ex-soldier in a wheelchair with only one arm slightly green; I shower all on my own, the other day I put the washing out on the line and only fell on the grass once. But the voice in my head is still coming to terms with the fact that I'm not the man I used to be. Ok, I was able to shower before but within five minutes, not fifteen and using one hand on the sink to steady myself whilst towelling dry.

Think of a middle-aged person who used to be amazing at Ultimate Frisbee (not 'Average' Frisbee but 'Ultimate' Frisbee) back at university. They keep themselves fairly fit over the years, no need for glasses or performance-enhancing drugs. A couple of decades on, someone asks them to stand in for the local Ultimate Frisbee team, 'this is my chance to prove I've still got it!' and – they're terrible. 'I used to be good at this! How dehumanising...'

There you go, the 'Ultimate' example.

THE AVOIDANCE PRINCIPLE

You don't prepare for this kind of thing, emotionally I mean. If someone reading this has recently had a worrying scan, or you think you might need looking at by someone medical, then take note; listen to your doctor/surgeon when they list all the terrible things they're going to do to you. Listen when they tell you your hair will fall out or you'll grow a third nipple (listen very carefully). Arm yourself with information, don't let anything take you by surprise and catch you off guard. Things are much harder to deal with if you don't see them coming.

Don't do what I did and pretend everything is ok upstairs. The isolation created by COVID-19 combined with cancer and the stress generated by the Toddler-Tornado I call my son, resulted in − avoidance. Avoidance of dealing with minor problems calmly, avoidance of sitting down and absorbing the impact of how my life was changing, avoidance of sensible human reactions to sensible human emotions − like sadness, regret or white-hot anger.

Keep your loved ones around you, or at least within arm's distance. My household most likely don't realise that I use them as an emotional crutch, they most likely see me as a closed book with the odd terrible joke. But without them dragging me back down to earth, I'd be lost in space.

MIRROR MIRROR ON THE WALL

I'm sorry to get 'real' all of a sudden (surprised myself a little as well) but physical symptoms are really only the tip of the iceberg. Yes, I'm not heading towards the Olympics, but society is much more accepting of physical deficiencies; not necessarily mental/emotional ones. I suppose this is a tribute to those struggling with mental health issues or just problems they'd rather not share with anyone.

If there's one thing you as the reader can take from this, it's this: every morning, get up, look in the mirror and ask one simple question – Am I ok?

The answer might very well be, 'yes'. Or it might not be. You deserve to ask yourself the question, because no-one else, not even your identical twin, can peer right into your soul and ask that question for you.

For me, my mental well-being is directly linked to my family. If they're fed up, I'm fed up. If my wife is in a bad mood (or 'awake') then I'm in a bad mood. Call me a Neanderthal but like most men I put all my emotional eggs in one basket, not delegating to the strong female archetype. Instead, I pigeonhole my problems in one place that I have easy access to. As opposed to opening several emotional bank accounts and compounding on the interest that way. Go figure.

ANGRY AT BEING ANGRY

I'm just so damn angry all the time. Just like Grumpy from Snow White and The Seven Dwarves, I seem to go looking for things to piss me off. I'm angry at my cancer. I'm angry at COVID-19. I'm angry at my friends and family for being nice to me. I'm angry at people in train stations with suitcases trailing two metres behind them, hell-bent on tripping people up as they look up at their platform number above. I'm angry at the idiot who lives on my road who has pebbles as his front drive, so I have to avoid them like landmines as I walk past. I'm angry at posh salt and vinegar crisps that have way too much damn vinegar on them.

I'm angry at being angry. It's not good for me, and it's starting to permeate my everyday thoughts. I feel like I want to punish the world, indiscriminately and in a selfish and childish way.

I sat on a bench in a park the other day with a memorial plaque. All I could think was that when I die, I want a bench erected in my name that has a bad design that forces you to sit with a bent back and a plaque that reads 'In memory of ****, who hated anyone that went on about their good posture.'

This just isn't healthy.

Farewell 'Witty Banter'

When there was no COVID-19 the last time I was recovering, I was able to meet with friends (honestly, I have actual human friends), or have people come visit the house. We didn't exactly sit there and analyse the content of my dreams, but just having people around me, became therapy.

That doesn't take anything away from the role my immediate family play; it's just a different experience speaking to a contemporary about something as inane as the weather, the state of the Brexit fiasco or Arsenal's chances of winning the Premier League once COVID-19 leaves (spoiler alert: it doesn't matter what year it is when you read these words, the chance is still almost zero).

I'm constantly told how well I'm doing, or that my voice sounds better, or that I look less like Frankenstein's monster since the last time we met. I truly appreciate that. I do. Maybe I am improving but, in my eyes, I'm moving as slowly as a glacier.

I don't think people are lying to my face, but I would like someone to speak their mind and come out with something like, 'damnit, what the hell are you doing, shuffling about like that? You look like you've been possessed by a ghost who's had a stroke! Why can't you speak more quickly? You sound like someone dropped a microphone into treacle.'

Well maybe not just like that, but when you have a personality that likes to give as good as you get, it's a big change having everyone suddenly be nice to you. I get nice messages from friends whom I would usually refer to as 'are you ok shit-for-brains?' or 'how's it going dick-head?', conversely being polite and asking about my health and family. I often try and reply with something witty and untrue like 'I'm struggling to walk properly but I managed to build a Nuclear Bunker in the garden should we hear anything else from North Korea.'

What I really want to communicate to them is what's really going on in my head. However, I fear that sending a recording of me screaming into my phone for five minutes wouldn't be admissible as 'witty banter'.

CHEMO BOY II - RETURN OF THE PILLS

I want to discuss the next step in my 'let's try every flavour of Tic-Tac to see if he responds' treatment plan. Take a note – lime and orange are the best.

Anyway, they may have been Tic-Tacs made to look like normal capsules but as far as my doctor was concerned, my next step was chemotherapy again. Last time round I had my 'lifetime dose' of radiotherapy to my brain and spine; the next time they'll try it will be if I'm so f**ked that they'll risk the drawbacks of more radiotherapy as opposed to treating me with nothing.

So yeah, more chemotherapy. My doctor commented that it was more than likely the first chemotherapy drugs had little to no effect on me, on account that my cancer came back so quickly. Therefore, I'm now on a very different treatment plan: I take one oral tablet, every day for five days in a row, every four weeks. So, for five days every month I take a tablet at home every day before I go to bed. The drug is called Temozolomide. As you can imagine, one of the most widely consumed poisons in the world (apart from 'Made in Chelsea') has its issues.

I'm under the directive to keep going with the chemo for at least six months and then see where we are, with a view to carry on for potentially years if my blood tests and side-effects are under control. There isn't really a situation where you say no to a request like that.

There's an illusion of consent and control we give to patients, but in reality, unless you're two hundred years old or you spend an hour each day perched precariously on the edge of a very high building, you're going to say 'yes please. I quite like being alive, I haven't watched all of Tiger King on Netflix yet'.

CHEMO COMPLICATIONS #1

Just a note here, I'm writing this quite early in my treatment plan, so my condition may change in time. So, here are some of the more minor, more common side-effects and I'll round it off with a couple of biggies. I don't want to list every side effect of every tablet I'm ever going to take, because that's just boring. However, in this case I think it paints a picture of what my life is like physically and what it easily could be, should I wander into more misfortune.

CHEMO COMPLICATIONS #2

Increased risk of bleeding. This is due to less platelets being made in the body and therefore not being sent to the areas in my body that need to stop bleeding – meaning I need to be careful around shaving or swallowing swords. Apparently, this is quite a common side effect, so I'll have monthly blood tests to nip this in the bud as early as possible.

Loss of appetite affected me big time a year ago. I would pause halfway through a meal, like a lion sensing nearby trouble. Only instead of stalking forward to battle I would slink off to go find a sick bowl. This year my appetite has so far been fine (except for when my wife eats tuna – Food of the Devil) and so therefore my weight has been ok. No nutritious milkshakes or thickeners.

Nausea/vomiting is a fairly common side effect of chemotherapy. As detailed before, nausea has been much less of an issue for me this time round, we'll have to see if future doses of chemo bring this unwelcome guest back home again and again. I'll be ready. Or at least my sick bowls will be.

Constipation or even diarrhoea. Ironic isn't it? Pretty much every potion prescribed has the potential to alter my perilously precarious bowel habits. I can't seem to catch a break. Back to Fibre Flakes for breakfast, I guess.

Tiredness and fatigue. Difficult to pin this one down to the tablets or not, there are many reasons for this one. Meds, yes. Two big operations, probably. Radiotherapy from ages ago, still possible. A lack of good exercise for over a year, certainly. As I've described before, being tired is not how you feel after ten minutes in the gym, staring into the mirror and polluting Instagram with pictures of your puny body.

Real fatigue is lumbering to the park behind your wife and child and when you get there, you beeline towards the nearest empty bench and – perch. You perch whilst you try and catch your breath as the world moves past you. Your son drops his pants in the middle of a field, starts to urinate in a circle and you're just too exhausted to shout out or call the police on the little toe-rag. Karma?

CHEMO COMPLICATIONS #3

Now let's look at the potentially more troublesome side effects. Or at least the ones more troublesome to me and my life. I've skipped loads of other side-effects, including hallucinations. Like a voice in my head asking, where am I? Why is this memoir so badly written? Why is Donald Trump in charge of nuclear weapons?

Firstly, I'm at risk of being immunocompromised and having low levels of white blood cells, the body's method of fighting off invading forces, i.e. I have an increased chance of getting an infection.

It's an almost distinctive feature of chemotherapy in today's society that people on it should not be around anything remotely infectious. You've seen the signs, 'not suitable for the elderly, pregnant, those on chemotherapy or anyone who thinks Emmerdale is a quality programme'.

In a nutshell, handle with care. Should I get the same infection as you, there's a damn good chance that you might get away with a mild illness or no symptoms at all, yet my body may struggle to recruit enough white blood cells to defend my own corner. And my outcome may be 'unfavourable'.

Similarly, there's an increased risk of me picking up and offloading an infection that normally wouldn't hang around, and therefore increases the risk of me knocking off poor Phyllis from down the road.

So maybe putting me in a giant sealed Zorb Ball isn't such a bad idea...

Practically this isn't great for a Children's doctor. Last year, my blood tests were almost back to normal by the time I bulldozed my way into work. I avoided the Intensive Care Unit with the sickest kids, and it was manageable. This time round I have no idea what the new chemotherapy drugs will do to my blood tests. I have no idea if I'll remain immunocompromised when I want to return to work. If I stay on these drugs for years, will there be a place for me in a hospital full of sick kids? Time will tell.

I've come out with it before, but I don't want this cancer to define me. I don't want it to be a secret either, I'm not ashamed and whispers behind your back are always worse when no-one knows the facts. Neither do I want to be known as 'Chemo Boy, don't touch him, you'll get SARS'. Ok, maybe people won't be like that, but it'll be hard to hide my health status when I'm not allowed on this ward, or I'm not allowed to use this piece of equipment or that one. People talk. It's basic human nature and you don't have to be Sherlock Holmes to work out details about people at work.

Practically, being on chemotherapy in the future will limit me. In some ways I'm yet to find out how it will, but alongside the infection risk and side-effects I've listed above, I could be dealing with this for years to come. And the alternative, if this chemotherapy doesn't work, is either another, potentially worse form of chemotherapy, or death. And then no more writing memoirs.

The second, and far more personal consequence of the chemotherapy, has affected me the most emotionally. It's a problem I'm not going to go into too much detail with because it's a concern that doesn't solely belong to me. It's something the British public find unsavoury to discuss verbally in depth, akin to describing whether or not you love your spouse or which of your children you'd offer first for human sacrifice.

Being on chemotherapy can either render you infertile or harm a baby whilst in the mother's womb. Effectively no babies whilst on the drug and not for some time after. Like I said, I'm not going to talk about my situation, other than detail what I can and can't have.

Put simply, I can maybe have children in the future. I may be rendered permanently infertile, I don't know. I definitely can't have children whilst on chemotherapy and a year after finishing.

Whatever happens, in this moment I have the most beautiful son in the world. My only concern is, in his world, Peppa F**king Pig has more influence than I do. I tell him not to throw something, he throws it. Peppa F**king Pig jumps in muddy puddles and all my son wants to do is jump in muddy puddles.

I want to take a tangent away from serious subjects and detail just how much I hate Peppa F**king Pig and my son's unrequited love of watching the TV show – Peppa F**king Pig is a selfish, demanding, rude, over-bearing and manipulative cretin of very low intelligence (even for a child) and has an annoying habit of dominating and ruining everyone's fun.

If you're an adult and you think Peppa F**king Pig presents a positive role model for your children, then you're like, totally, like, stupid.

You'd never have guessed that I've been forced to watch all three hundred and three episodes with the boy...

I don't know if I'm allowed to put webpage links but have a go at this one, it's like whoever authored this website shares my hatred for Peppa F**king Pig and lived inside my brain for a while:

https://peppafanon.fandom.com/wiki/Home

GENETIC ERROR OR DIVINE RETRIBUTION

Now let me talk about something that I don't mind going into detail, despite it being a bit touchy. It all started from the first tumour where my wife asked my Oncologist about the Genetics. Basically, is this tumour an indication of a genetic problem, or a syndrome? It's a more pertinent question if the patient is young and the tumour is rare. Like someone I know.

At the time, based on examining the tumour they fished out the back of my head, it was deemed to be a **somatic** genetic mutation, which means it's random and affects the cells of the body **after** you're born. To be clear, it could be because you smoked a thousand cigarettes a day, drank a litre of whiskey every morning or worked in an asbestos factory. Or, it could be plain bad luck, a random distortion of genetic code picked up in later life, resulting in a biological anomaly, or a mistake of nature. Just like any individual that appears on Love Island. Although you could easily argue they were born brain-less and there's nothing random about it....

The other type of genetic mutation is **germline**, which means the cells that resulted in your cancer/terrible personality were changed whilst mixing in the fertilisation stage, or **before** birth. You inherit these dodgy mutations from one or both parents. This means you can pass it on to your children, one or more of your siblings may be affected or any change may have skipped one or multiple generations. Basically, you could be unlucky and inherit some isolated, weird genetic mutation from one parent or, you could be really unlucky and inherit a genetic syndrome that can affect multiple members of your family.

The syndrome potentially linked to my cancer is called Li Fraumeni syndrome. It's a very rare disorder that results in an increased overall risk of cancer within your lifetime and also gives you cancer earlier in life. Essentially there's a gene in the body that suppresses or holds off tumour cell production. In Li Fraumeni syndrome this gene goes on strike and allows the body to produce cancer cells in surplus, like an abysmal Disney sequel film that no-one wants (I'm looking at you, The Little Mermaid 2).

It gives you various types of cancer before old age and, more alarmingly, results in cancer for children. The age expectancy is, err, low. As far as me and my wife were concerned, it was a death sentence for me, our son and potentially both my parents and my brother.

***

At the beginning of this year my Oncologist asked us if we wanted to see a geneticist to further explore the possibility that I could have the syndrome or not. We said yes, expecting to be told that this was a waste of time and that there was no way I could have this condition. The rarity and type of my cancer, plus the genetic mutation they found on analysing my first tumour, fitted with a possible diagnosis of Li Fraumeni syndrome.

The genetic clinic is one I've had professional contact with for years, mainly to refer children with barn-door genetic problems and their parents are first cousins or massively over-familiar siblings. I didn't expect to find myself there... I wasn't embarrassed, it just felt a bit like when a policeman falls from grace and lands in prison amongst the punters he put there.

So, into the clinic room we went (with a medical student present to potentially witness some more human tragedy, not the same student as before, that would have been weird). The doctor asked for a brief run-through of the story and asked me numerous questions about my family tree. She then outlined how horrific Li Fraumeni was and how we were going to rule it in or out. Essentially a single blood test to look for that particular gene and determine if it was somatic or germline.

Then came the most important question from the doctor – do you want to know the result? This seemed an odd question to me until she outlined very clearly what it would mean to receive the result, either way. A negative (or somatic) result would mean we all go home fairly happy that we've ruled out a potentially fatal syndrome.

A positive or partly positive result would leave us in a state of flux, still not 100% sure it's a syndrome, but pretty sure somebody in my family would get cancer in their lifetime, potentially anytime soon. This would result in yearly or even six-monthly scans, maybe other tests, not sure. It would almost certainly result in my early death.

The main reason I was asked 'do you want to know the result?' is not necessarily regarding the state of my health, I couldn't give less of a shit about my life when considering the other implications of having the syndrome. When asked 'do you want to know the result?' I'm essentially having to make the decision if it's a positive result – do I tell my family that they're potentially going to die of cancer at an early age?

Maybe they already have a cancer in their body, lying dormant. My brother is in his twenties, he may not see thirty if he does have the syndrome. Knowledge of potentially having the syndrome but having nothing wrong with you would be worrying enough, but they would be offered yearly or maybe more frequent scans, which is worrying in itself. Every appointment with a doctor would be like the beginning of a horror film: 'will today be the day I'm told I have cancer?'

***

You may have guessed it but the main reason to be anxious was because of my son. Sorry, not anxious, terrified. The way the genetic mutation works is if I have the syndrome, then there's a one in two chance my son has it. That would mean frequent scans and tests for a toddler that has no idea what's going on. Potentially for life, and a damn high chance of getting cancer in childhood, not 'early' in adulthood like me.

Imagine as a parent going to a hospital appointment and being told your child has months to live, or that they're going to have to have radical surgery or chemotherapy and they'll be in horrific pain. I'd give both my arms to avoid even one minute of pain for my son, much less a condition like mine, before his life has even really begun.

Those that believe this is some sort of celestial edict and that a child being in that kind of position is fated to be so; they can shove their sanctimonious head up their arse and go play in traffic. There's nothing positive about any of this. Whilst waiting for the results of my blood test I would lie in bed every night and think about it for a minute or so. The pain I would feel just by imagining the situation would spread across my body like wildfire, abating only when I could convince my mind to focus on something else. Then I'd wake up. And think about him again.

I'll not beat about the bush anymore, my wife and I had to wait over three excruciating months to hear the result. It came in the form of a phone call that I answered on my smartwatch because my phone was downstairs. Not the best way to receive any news really... A female doctor's voice floated from my wrist: 'the test is negative; this is good news!'

And that was it. No more scary syndrome thoughts. What do I agonise about now?

LOOKING BACK ON ME, LOOKING BACK

Can I do more self-reflection at this point? Was I wrong to belittle the concept at medical school? Label the act of looking back and analysing my feelings and behaviour as something only people who have really screwed up do? Was I wrong to shove this section towards the end after all the more interesting bits? We're taught to reflect as we go, I worry that I tend to roll down the Hill of Life, land in a heap and then look quizzically up the side of the hill, 'how did I get here? Why am I naked?'

I looked back over Part One of this memoir to reflect on what I was reflecting on before. Reading it over for me was like listening to a recording of my voice. What is that whiny little bitch going on about? He should just get on with it and stop using naughty words to mask his inadequacies with language. He should.

And he could, if only life would stop throwing curveballs at him. I asked myself if I'd changed as a person, possibly the most pertinent question I could ask myself. I think I have an answer now, whereas before I mainly threw the question back, almost rhetorically. I think my outlook on life has become more fatalistic, but really, I feel like the same old soul, maybe just in a slightly older and more broken vessel.

I may come across more frustrated and rageful, but I think that aligns itself with my current physical situation. That can change, the world can change. But you don't change your family, or your values. I think it'll take ten brain tumours to change my views of my son having a ponytail. Or a nose piercing. Or become a Tottenham fan.

I previously said how lucky I am to be alive, that sentiment hasn't changed and right now my perspective is shifted by just how many deaths there are in the world due to COVID-19. This led me to thinking, would I be better off dead with no physical effects or dependencies? As opposed to my life now, alive but full of resentment and rhetoric? Can I complain about constipation when someone's grandmother has died in a nearby hospital, and I'm sat here moaning into my laptop?

Well yes, yes I can, but I'm not especially proud of it. My problems are everything to me, my outlook on life right now may well be bleak and pessimistic – but I shouldn't forget the days I wake up and my son jumps on me in bed and kisses me. I shouldn't forget the days I look at my wife's face and realise there's no man on this earth that's as lucky as me. I shouldn't forget the days where I help bring a child out of illness and misery and back into full health.

And the only way to have those kinds of experiences, is to survive, at all costs.

Is This the End?

Is this the end? The end of my memoir I mean, not the Apocalypse or the last episode of The Great British Bake Off. My adventure continues of course, monthly chemotherapy, frequent scans, blood tests and Confessionals to the priest.

To be as grim and morbid as possible, I often think about my legacy, or what I'll leave behind once I'm dead. I'm young, medically speaking, but the universe seems to be trying it's hardest to cut short my one and only performance. Will I leave a positive model for my son? Keep going no matter what tries to slow you down? Be rude to people then claim it's because of a brain tumour? Or will my memory be one of regret, especially if I go too early?

I'm reminded of a fantastic ancient Greek proverb; 'old men plant trees, the shade of which they know they will never sit in'. Should I be planting trees of knowledge and wisdom for my son to enjoy before I check out? This proverb is, in my opinion, immortalised in Ricky Gervais' excellent dark comedy, 'Afterlife', where it reverberated around my head for hours, forcing me to think and reflect on what I can do to change the world for my son.

Financial security? Working on it. Social security? Working on it. Emotional security? Might be above my paygrade, but I'm working on it. I guess I've written this so when he's older and reading this, it may form part of some sort of legacy, I don't know.

PERSPECTIVE

In a way I've enjoyed putting this down on paper. I've enjoyed sharing my toils and troubles with the page in a way I know I can't with another human being. I'm going to echo what I said before; I hope this account helps someone gain perspective on their illness or even a life like mine in general, either through laughter or shock and horror. I'm not trying to be sensationalist, I truly hate Peppa F**king Pig and I did get cancer, twice. Nothing is untrue (unless I've very clearly said it is) and if you think I've rabbited on about a particular topic too much, it's probably because it holds such significance in my little corner of the world.

The act of writing this has helped. I've been told a problem shared is a problem halved (I think that's how it goes) and so sharing this may have benefited me just as much as you. I have a way to go on my journey, I hope, and there's definitely room to grow. I sincerely hope to never have to visit this place again. Unless someone reads this and points out a spelling error. Then I won't sleep for a while.

LET'S TRY AND BE GOOD

As a final thought, have I exited my cocoon as a good man? Yes, I'm aware I have too much gut to fit in any size cocoon and there's hopefully a good way to go in this story. However, in this short period a lot has happened to me, I'm certainly not the man I was before, and maybe I never was the monster I portrayed that takes cheap shots at people that can't defend themselves or tries to hurt those around me. Maybe it was the operation, the meds or even The Spanish Inquisition (another Monty Python sketch, Google it please)!

I was joking about laughing at fat people or running over old ladies in my car, I have less than admirable thoughts, yes, but I mainly use humour as a screen with which to hide my insecurities behind. I love my family and those around me and would eagerly suffer another day of cancer if it meant one more day of happiness for my son.

My work is helping children, I see no point in it if I can't make children happy. My writing is hopefully going to help someone, with any luck. I don't like to go to bed without making at least one person happy in that day, or even just getting a smile.

Maybe there is some good in me, mixed in with all the rage and restlessness.

One day I'll talk to my son about my experiences and I truly hope at the end of it I'll come out as a good man. It would be easy to paint myself as a victim but there's more to illness than that. There's the way you deal with it, from the simple act of lying to your wife that you don't feel sick to make her a tiny bit happier, to the motivation or drive to do something with your time that will help the most people you can. Like get back to work or bake biscuits or whatever.

There's also the way you perceive it. I've talked about my anger and resentment, frustration that this could happen to me in such a random way. And it is random, it's no-one else's fault and I certainly didn't ask for it. But I think I'm slowly coming around to the idea that those emotions will only take me so far. I have to use the time I have left to teach my son to use that negative energy and transform it into something positive, to try and help others, and to one day become a truly good man.

PART 3

FOREWORD #3/APPALLING APPENDIX

I think, I may be a good man after all, dressed as a wolf, in sheep's clothing. Not sinister, like the Biblical wolf reference; there may yet be a fairly decent showing of my inner, warm and fluffy sheep to be discovered. Maybe.

I think some of the conclusions and realisations that I've come to about the people around me, have led me astray from my familiar, more comfortable path of melancholy. I think this is leading me meandering slowly towards much calmer waters. This is making me pretty nervous.

Don't get me wrong, I haven't changed that much, I still have murderous feelings about people who don't hurry the last few steps when you hold the door open for them, people that stop their car ten metres away from the traffic light for no good reason, or people that don't recognise the genius of every Jason Statham film ever made. I haven't lost my damn mind whilst borrowing some of the world's empathy and compassion.

I've decided not to drag this section of my life through the murky, muddy, mire of proper memoir tale-telling; I'm going to lump this into a shortish appendix, despite it being very much a foreword to the third round of my cancer woes.

THIRD TIME LUCKY

Ten points to Gryffindor, my cancer came back again. Again.

Similar place in my brain, the last chemotherapy turned out to be as much use as a chocolate teapot and so my tumour grew slowly and silently into the brain cavity previously inhabited by my previous cancer. No new symptoms or premonitions, just a disappointing scan result.

My father helpfully described my third cancer diagnosis as 'Third time lucky'. Third time lucky for who? As in Third time the last time? Or Third time the last time he has to put up with my presence at Christmas or Birthdays???

I certainly don't think I'm 'Third time lucky'. What do you think?

There must be a fantastical Classical reference to describe my latest tumour growing in the wake of its ancestor. I just can't think of one and common protocol and courtesy would dictate I spend a long time trying to find the best example. But I'm much too busy swimming in the lake of my new-found positivity. So, I'm just going to chalk it down to rotten, yet poetic, bad luck.

THE SULTAN OF SOLILOQUY

I need a new uplifting soliloquy (in a book yes, not in a play like it should be - it's not lost on me, I just really enjoy that word) about where my head is at the time of writing.

Personally, I think the last few paragraphs of Part Two weren't half bad; it was truly sincere, not just aimed for the Hollywood trilogy of films I can see people queuing up for outside the house. Plus, it came from my black, twisted heart. All of it.

I didn't expect to live this long, and so I think I've covered a lot of personal issues already, in anticipation of the much-anticipated End of Days, my Foreboded Prognosticated Sentencing – basically I thought I could squeeze in a few more thoughts before I Popped my Clogs. Now I'm sat here with my pants around my ankles, still alive, trying to attach some more heartfelt sentiment to something I didn't expect or wish to see again.

But try I will, because the act of looking into myself for answers gives me real hope that there may be a similar process for anyone out there reading this.

FREAKS AND GEEKS

I've thought about my perception of myself then (Before Cancer) and now (Anno Canceri (I've made this up, I've checked, don't worry)). Or to look at it a different way, what I put myself forward as now and what I put myself forward as before.

Freaks and Geeks.

And I don't mind if you jump to conclusions about where I'm headed, although you'd be wrong. I'm not referring to the weird middle-aged man shuffling around your local park with a hair lip and a mysterious limp, furtively escorting a deck of Pokémon cards aboard a Hello Kitty backpack.

I'm talking about one of my favourite Childish Gambino tracks of the same name. His enigmatic delivery of the idea that there are those in society that don't fit in or conform to the Status Quo - and you don't have to conform, you don't have to behave the way people on 'Love Island', or 'Lord of the Flies' behave. You can have a hair lip or a mysterious limp, knock yourself out.

Ok, maybe the song isn't exactly about people with medical conditions struggling in society, but it's my interpretation that counts here.

***

Let me try and explain; during my time in the Cancer Hospital, the Neurology ward and generally being out and about, I've come across multiple characters with gross neurological problems affecting their appearance, behaviour and even personality. I did my level best to avoid them during my travels, did my best to sneak past their rooms when the fireworks started, did my best to hide behind myself.

My own experiences of appearing 'different' in today's world may appear much more subtlety than some of the more visible displays I've witnessed in others; people reply to my long queries with 'eh?' still, so I slow my speech down and 'enunciate' (felt like I had to highlight this fantastic word).

When I walk in a straight line I might occasionally buckle or even straighten one of my legs, leading me to stagger and give the impression I'm about to kiss the pavement – more than once a passing stranger has reacted and shifted their balance, I assume to help me should I fall, but you never know. Luckily, through time and practice, I have a very good straighten-up-after-I-wobble technique that means I've never fallen over in front of people. I just kind of brush myself off and stagger on, staring straight ahead and trying not to achieve eye contact with my would-be saviour, both of us a little embarrassed at the almost-accident. Odd looks in my direction as I hold onto my wife's arm, 'Nothing to see here!'

On reflection, this is all a problem for me, not for anyone else. Most people don't point and laugh at me or throw rotten vegetables. I can't predict or understand the thoughts of others, so my issues are all within my own perception.

Some individuals may think that they're much better or worse off than I am, I don't know. I know I'm describing us as Freaks and Geeks collectively, because of how I view myself, not anyone else really. I've callously clumped these unfortunate individuals into the same mental prison that I find myself in. And they may well not belong anywhere near me, it's how you feel inside, not where society places you.

At the same time, they are my Freaks and Geeks. I'm their Freak, I'm their Geek. I'm their equal in the respect that we may or may not be exactly where we want to be at this point in time, or where/how we want to be placed in society. I'm not being overly depressive, I think I'm just acknowledging my current situation, and not moping about the past.

I know now, that what makes me different, doesn't always ostracise me. It's just that my mind and body aren't exactly playing together nicely right now, and positivity aside, there's a part of me that feels the world and The Fates are against me. That feeling may never dissipate until my first Olympic medal.

We may not be at 110% presently, but alongside a pile of performance-enhancing drugs and Pixie Dust, there's nothing Freaks and Geeks can't accomplish in this world.

WHOEVER YOU ARE, SOME PART OF ME LOVES YOU

So, I'm going to stop now. No more. I wanted to be a rebellious youth and end this messily and write something horrific that would prevent my mother from ever speaking to me again, but that can wait till my funeral eulogy (hint to the eulogy author: feel free to use the word 'Adonis' whenever you can).

Alas, I'm no longer rebellious and I certainly don't feel youthful anymore.

Therefore, I just want to say thank you to all the people who have helped keep me alive up till now. All the people who have kept a smile on my face. All the people that have sat there and absorbed my volleys of verbal venom, never complaining. All the people that have allowed me to be me, and maybe even a better, wiser version of me.

I mean this in the sincerest sense imaginable. Thank you.

***

Cancer is a horrible thing. There's very little good that comes of it. It changes us, alters our sense of being and forces us to re-evaluate our place in this world and the places we imagine ourselves to be in in the future.

That's just the way it is.

So, I'm going to be the next best thing I can be right now. Not what would be expected of me as a result of having cancer, but the best version of me, I can be.

I don't know who you are, but if I can do it, then you can do it.

A Message From Naomi

Unfortunately Aria's health deteriorated just before publication of his memoir, and so I have been left with writing a little message on his behalf. I wish I could write something smart and witty but unfortunately I'm not as talented as Aria when it comes to literacy.

So I'll keep it short and sweet, Aria wrote this memoir with the hope for it to be real, relatable, raw and at the same time funny. It's aimed for anyone who has been touched by cancer in one form of another (which I think will be most people). If all you take from it is to love, be kind and live life to the full he will be happy.

Aria has also written two Childrens books titled; Eddie and the Magic Healing Stone, and Eddie and the Last Dodo On Earth. The proceeds will go to various charities including Brain Tumour Research and also charities which have helped us personally and are eternally grateful for; including the Royal Medical Foundation, Society for Assistance of Medical Families and Royal Medical Benevolent Fund.

Stay safe be kind and live life.

Naomi

BV - #0033 - 151021 - C0 - 210/148/10 - PB - 9781914151071 - Gloss Lamination